HOOFING ON
BROADWAY

HOOFING ON BROADWAY

A History of Show Dancing

RICHARD KISLAN

PRENTICE HALL PRESS • NEW YORK

Published by Prentice Hall Press
A Division of Simon & Schuster, Inc.
Gulf+Western Building
One Gulf+Western Plaza
New York, NY 10023

PRENTICE HALL PRESS is a trademark of Simon & Schuster, Inc.

Library of Congress Cataloging-in-Publication Data

Kislan, Richard.
   Hoofing on Broadway.

   Includes index.
   1. Dancing—United States—History. 2. Musical revue,
comedy, etc.—United States—History. I. Title.
GV1623.K57 1986   792.3′2′0973   86-18757
ISBN 0-13-809484-5

Manufactured in the United States of America

Designed by Publishing Synthesis Ltd.

1 3 5 7 9 10 8 6 4 2

First Edition

CONTENTS

PREFACE

Nothing in the American musical theater has been more inaccessible to its public than the record of its dance tradition. Our musical-theater literature has been around for years—frozen in print or musical notes, catalogued with care, or assembled in the scrapbook and clipping files of libraries already rich in librettos and scores, pictorial surveys, and the memoirs of popular stars. So preserved, the literary tradition of our lyric theater rests comfortably, safe from the ravages of time. But fate extended no such courtesy to the performance tradition of musical-theater dance.

The inequity stems from the very nature of dance as an ephemeral art traditionally passed on from generation to generation by demonstration, imitation, practice, and personal supervision. Consequently, the vast majority of American musicals danced across the nation's stages without a record on film or videotape to preserve the sights and sounds of their dynamic life, or a notation system to monitor their pulse. Dancers and dancing figured prominently on the American musical stage from the very beginning. Yet, for the most part, the dance movement itself was either the last to be mentioned by critics or, more often, ignored altogether. Although musicals on the American stage had been alive and well for more than two hundred years, no permanent notation of a show's complete choreography existed until *Bye Bye Birdie* (1960) was recorded in the Labanotation system (a written system for notating movements in dances). What pictorial records survive from earlier periods freeze but one second of the dance combination in time—one pose pulled from what was once a continuous, living, moving experience. Much has been lost, and lost forever. So, if we are to continue to acknowledge a tradition of musical theater in America, no influential aspect of that tradition should be neglected. Just as The American Dance Machine (dance company and living archive) is committed to the preservation of the choreography of important musicals for study by dancers, so too should a comprehensive study of that tradition—through its movement and its dancers—be available in print to guide its teachers, nourish its scholars, and inform and entertain the public. What our musical stage is today is in large measure the result of more than two centuries of being and becoming. Now is the time to demonstrate in print the inherent nature, range and scope, and unbroken continuity of dance expression in our commercial musical theater.

Picture American show dance as a giant but fragile cornucopia—giant, in that it encloses a vast and richly diverse variety of people, events, ideas, trends, and styles; fragile, because, like music, dance performance exists in time as kinesthetic images that pass us and are gone forever. To begin to understand this marvelous and elusive phenomenon, we must first search out its history, discover its genesis, and examine the course it traveled to its present prominence in the modern musical. Far from being modern phenomena, today's musical shows share a legacy inherited from the eighteenth century, and dance and prescribed stage movement have been integral parts of that legacy from the very beginning. At first, theater dances drew on and reflected the social dances of their time and place. Later, indigenous influences from plantation, country, and frontier sources led to the characteristically American steps and styles—that unique combination of jazz and ethnic elements that has come to be known as Broadway dance—that has created generations of Broadway dancers—and that, by universal consensus, accounts for much of the energy and vibrant personality of the modern musical. The first part of this book explores this phenomenon.

With the mid-twentieth-century maturation of the American musical theater came a concomitant intensification of its dances and of the sophistication of its dancers. The second part of the book reflects this development by focusing on an aesthetic appreciation of those artists who set the standards, prescribed the direction, and thereby secured the conspicuous place of movement and dance on our musical stage. First came the visionaries who guided the ship of dance into uncharted territory. Then came the masters who steered its passage within already prescribed and accepted conventions. Following them are the contemporary masterminds whose reputation and achievements dominate the "dance biz" of today's show biz and whose principal work defines the state of dance art for our commercial musical theater. To them we attribute the recent vogue for musicals that move, the prominence of directors who choreograph, and the sudden expansion of performance opportunities for dancers who also sing and act.

Ideas and practices in American theater dance are celebrated in the final section of the book. To succeed within the broader context of a musical show, movement and dance must be agreeably functional; that is, they must be complete and enjoyable in themselves while simultaneously supporting some broader theatrical design. All who dance celebrate movement; those who dance in the lyric theater pursue purposeful movement. Consequently, the best dances on our musical stage invite critical observation, scrutiny, and analysis. They group into types and styles; extend the theatrical functionality of pieces; prefer certain musical arrangements and orchestrations; profit from responsive sets, lighting, and costumes, and require exhaustive training to be danced properly. Like other organisms, theater dance can be dissected, studied, and reassembled in order to determine its nature and examine significant relationships among its principal parts.

A few words of warning: However well intended, any account of a living movement tradition can only approximate the dynamic performance itself. On stage, dance performances live through the peculiar flesh and energy applied by individual bodies to script and score. The performance itself should be the central concern of all who really care for the American musical theater. However, if economy or geography intervenes, this book will exist to help reconstruct dance performances, and the dynamic personalities of those who created and performed them, in the theater of the imagination. Or, when fancy succumbs to more practical considerations, the text may be used as a reference or guide or as a first step into the personal experience of the world of show dancing. As our modern director-choreographers make increasing use of all parts of the stage—even to the extent of choreographing the scenery—it becomes incumbent on the interested public to develop a kinesthetic perception of what is happening; that is, a refined dynamic memory able to perceive, remember, and appreciate the continuous flow of movement within the choreographic design. At today's prices, the audience should be ready to come to terms with what they're paying for.

If today's musical theater book is the fountain from which a show's creative waters spring, and if its songs embody the life of a culture in a given time and place, then movement and dance represent the living pulsebeat of a live theater performance. A living line of movement and dance extends to us from the earliest periods of musical theater activity in America. It is up to us to reach out and secure our moorings now.

INTRODUCTION

A STAGE DANCE TRADITION

We live in a visual age. Technology allows us to watch our leaders and our wars, royal weddings and championship games, natural disasters and the latest action on MTV. The virtually unavoidable pervasiveness of television, movies, and video and the acknowledged emphasis on the viewed experience over what might be read, heard, or imagined have so intensified the American public's appetite for visual stimulation that no one communications industry can put up sufficient collateral to satisfy the demand. In addition, the current trend toward physical fitness and healthful living, combined with the social premium on slim, tight bodies that radiate overall physical attractiveness, has brought about an ideal climate for an appreciation of and participation in exercise, sports, and dance. Not by coincidence has dance developed into our nation's most vigorous and multidimensional performing art. And of all the persuasions that make up the contemporary dance scene, guess which one is most visible, marketable, and popular? What do *Flashdance, A Chorus Line,* a Michael Jackson video, *Footloose,* any number of television commercials, and Fred Astaire have in common? You guessed it! American show dance.

While show dancing has always been popular on the American stage, its present ascendancy may be attributed to a true and deep artistic need to turn away from the written and spoken language that has generated so many of the lies of our time and make contact again with the more honest, primitive, and universal language that genuinely motivated movement affords. All who have encountered the promises of politicians, the contradictory claims of rival nations, or the just plain deception by a loved one know that in each case, the culprit, the agent of deception, has been words. To that public—those who no longer spontaneously believe what is said or trust what is read—the incorruptible messages of the body represent an alternative form of communication to be cherished in life, sought after in popular entertainment, and understood, valued, and encouraged in theatrical art. As one canny observer, contemporary scholar Louis Jeriel Summers, has noted, "You can talk out of the side of your mouth but you can't dance out of the side of your mouth."

In the recent American musical theater, a growing awareness of the potential power, scope, and universality of stage dancing has revolutionized the way musicals are conceived and created, as well as how performers function in them. Growing, too, is an awareness that modern audiences respond best to shows that move. With the exception of the brilliant, visionary, and predictably unpredictable efforts of Stephen Sondheim and his collaborators, major revivals, and "let's-take-a-step-backward-play-it-safe-and-sell-some-tickets" productions, the rise or fall of the modern Broadway musical has come to depend less on the quality of work produced by author, lyricist, and composer than on the creative energy, craft, and professional know-how of the leading director-choreographers. There are reasons—Broadway economics; the accelerating exodus of promising writers and musicians to Madison Avenue, movies, television, and the record industry; and the generally perceived tendency of the times to value style over substance, charisma over content, and delivery of data over the data itself. Although a good many scholars bemoan the disappearance of the popular musical as a writer's medium, the inescapable fact remains: The merchants of movement now occupy the driver's seat on the commercial musical's philosophical, creative, and professional journey to a Broadway opening. For performers, these dance- and movement-oriented shows inflate the importance of kinetic skills for anyone hoping to be cast. Gone are the days of a chorus whose constituents could do little more than pose decorously and parade in unison around the stage. The professional careers of singers who expect to dissolve into a comfortable, static background during today's production numbers will fizzle, as will the careers of dancers who can only dance and actors with no aptitude in song and dance. The total performance versatility that once embodied an elusive ideal has become today's minimum requirement for jobs in shows like *A Chorus Line, Dreamgirls,* and *Cats.* That yesterday's exception became today's rule underscores the tremendous technical improvements achieved in recent years by the aspiring Broadway chorus performer. Yet, unlike questionable acting skills that an experienced director can camouflage effectively in an already abbreviated musical book, or a weak singing voice that the now-indispensable sound technician can easily amplify, little or no faculty for dance represents a serious and virtually irredeemable drawback. Either you leap, you turn, you move to the rhythm—or you do not. Kinetic ineptitude cannot be disguised; routine mistakes cannot be hidden. What choreographer about to be reviewed by the *New York Times* can afford to stage all the dances in darkness, fog, or behind the set?

Tremendous improvements in the kinetic perceptivity of modern audiences severely limit the choreographer's options for concealing a dancer's liabilities. Nor can one pass off an obvious ugly duckling as a possible swan to an audience that has already logged countless hours before the television set watching the bodies beautiful—all fitness and form—run, jump, reach, dive, vault, and dance ballet, jazz, or disco just for us in the privacy of our homes. Can we fault modern audiences for expecting the same or better from a handsomely priced stage production? Consequently, the new equation for American stage dance reads: Inflated audience expectations beget higher standards; higher standards elicit better training; better training fuels the virtuosic demands of choreographers who accept current achievements and aspire to stretch themselves and their dancers with each new project. No wonder the most consistent accomplishments of recent Broadway musicals belong to the director-choreographers. So vital has been their contribution that, with the 1976 revised copyright act, choreography and pantomime were finally designated as subject matter suitable for copyright in the United States. Prior to January 1, 1978, when the new law went into effect, commercial theater choreography could only be protected from unauthorized performances if the choreographer succeeded in registering the work as a dramatic composition.

Dance for the popular stage in America boasts a long and colorful tradition, one that predates as well as absorbs ballet, modern dance, and jazz, ballroom, ethnic, disco, and street dancing. Within each idiom evidence of different dance types, techniques, ideas, values, steps, and trends appears. Specific dance elements appear and reappear with surprising regularity over a span of two centuries, at times reproduced faithfully in major revivals or, as in current practice, assimilated into the personal styles of choreographic artists who have a sense of the past as well as the present. *Pippin, A Chorus Line, Ballroom,* and *Barnum* represent decidedly modern treatments of movement and dance material from the past. Philosophically speaking, American stage dance enjoys both a linear tradition with an ebb and flow of trends, historical influences, and artistic accomplishments as well as a tradition of vertical integration in which varied and often irreconcilable forms coexist simultaneously—as concert dance, ballet, modern, jazz, and tap prevail as exclusive artistic entities with their own tradition, training, repertory, and audience. The American show dance tradition embraces them all, often with several types of dance appearing in a single show. Choreographic viewpoint submits to this vertical integration as well. Choreographers whose overriding intent is to astonish with physical eccentricity or virtuosic display coexist with those intent on the artistic exploration of movement as dramatic and theatrical metaphor. To look back over the two hundred years of show dance in America is to see unity formed out of diversity. In the hospitable climate of American popular entertainment, a very hardy, adaptable, and successful species of dance and dancer evolved from what Jack Cole referred to as dance "wallpaper" into the most sophisticated modern manifestation of dance not merely as integral support for the dramatic event but as the dramatic event itself.

"Show dance." "Stage dance." "Commercial dance." While each term implies allegiance to the same tradition, minor variations based on the distinctions among the various branches of show business allow for a more specific application of each term. The term "show dance" gives us the most comprehensive name by which the product of its tradition is known. The business of "show," as in "show business," refers to the process of putting in sight or view and thus causing to appear or to be seen. When applied to dance, the term "show" would cover all popular entertainment that employs movement and dance. The term "commercial dance" encourages comprehensive application as well, suggesting as it does dancing for money (as in popular entertainment) as distinct from dancing for art (as in modern and avant-garde dance). Use of the term "stage dance" should be limited to the dancing that appears in the theater, but if a common denominator exists among the diverse manifestations of show dance, then what are its properties, characteristics, styles, functions, and standards? Where and when did it originate? How did it develop? Let's begin with a definition. Show dance is a convention of body movement drawn from a variety of sources and applied to commercial entertainments for the purpose of artistic communication, unabashed diversion, or both. As in science, where the terms "pure" and "applied" operate, so with dance. Show dance is not pure dance but applied dance; that is, a body of movement language put to practical use in a variety of media and in which dancers execute steps and combinations within a design from which the audience is meant to interpret an idea, emotion, or mood. This expressive movement should not be interpreted solely in terms of what it means for the dancer, choreographer, or viewer, but always in relation to what appears to be intended within the context of the commercial property in which it appears. The language of show dancing is not precise. It communicates with kinetic symbols whose meaning derives from a specific context to which the choreographer appends a statement fashioned on the bodies of the dancers. Even the most outrageous specialty acts of vaudeville responded to a purpose within the immoderately competitive context that forced performers to distinguish their acts from all others on the circuit. In the most advanced application of show dance in musical plays and musical comedy, kinetic images happen for and because of their extraordinary dramatic and theatrical functions. In an applied art, no serious commercial performer can afford to risk the unpredictable, unintended, or haphazard before even the most provincial of audiences. To the gifted, the sensitive, and the intellectually acute, the seeming restraints of purpose and function provide an artistic road map that guides the choreographer or dancer during the journey from self to audience. If the audience must be made to understand something, or just to feel or to be encompassed by a mood, then the choreographer must recognize that obligation at the earliest stages of the creative process, direct all energies and material to the realization of that objective, and inhibit any inclination to create dances for self-aggrandizement, psychological release, or public notoriety. In the late eighteenth and early nineteenth centuries, managers used show dance for incidental diversion: olios between acts to placate the customers, specialty routines to exploit a star's celebrity, or pantomime and ballet to titillate predominantly male audiences with the alluring spectacle of female limbs in tights. By the 1940s, applied dance had achieved recognized artistic status; it revealed character, theme, thought, and feeling; it made dramatic action visible and revealed plot faster than the speed of the words of a scene, as it determined the pace of an evening's entertainment. Formerly a decidedly secondary element in the mix of dialogue, song, and dance, dance now replaces dialogue and often absorbs song. Unfortunately, the major milestones on so considerable a journey remain unrecorded in Labanotation, film, and video. Dance is an ephemeral art; show dance is the most ephemeral part of an ephemeral whole.

American show dance *is* because it borrows; American show dance *is* because it is vulgar. What else can you expect from an activity committed to audience impact and devoted to audience approval? The American musical theater itself has always been a popular theater that caters to the preferences of a melting-pot population. So must its components be. Vulgarity allows for sexual suggestiveness, anatomical exhibition, and even nudity; but it packs the house, and that's what counts for the life of a show. Besides, if theater people produce musical shows to reach out to the very last person in the last row of the balcony, then it is in the spirit of the creative proceedings not to hold back but rather to thrust out concept, soul and body. Not surprisingly, the history of popular American entertainment is littered with the names of show dancers who scandalized contemporaries to the considerable profit of their managers.

The more things change, the more they remain the same. Then, audiences flocked to the hootchy-kootchy, the shimmy, and the strip-tease; today, audiences flock to the latest offering from the Jack Cole/Bob Fosse approach to earthly delights. Clearly, the history of American stage dance constitutes a record of American social acceptance of that delight in the bodies of dancers. Throughout our history, enterprising managers (down to the dullest among them) realized that vulgar stage dance usually attracts the largest audience. There has always been a market for instant gratification in the United States. As shown dance strives to market its wares to an ever-increasing audience, it has embraced the character of an occupational activity. Face it, as have generations of American dancers: *Show dance is a job.* Since it's a highly competitive job, its power brokers tend to favor looks, body type, sex appeal, and personality. Today, everybody in serious contention has a technique. In show business, a dancer must have something to show. If not, the complaint is familiar: "Dance: Ten. Looks: Three."

For the choreographer, the show-dancing milieu offers some major artistic liabilities. The major creative handicap is this: In the majority of shows produced for the commercial stage, ideas, form, and perfor-mance values originate with the writers. In its pure form, dance partakes of both origination (creation) and performance (interpretation). In pure dance, the choreographer is king; all praise and damnation be his. Some contemporary superstar director-choreographers may indeed enjoy the ideal: total control over book, lyrics, score, and production in a commer-cial show business venture. Michael Bennett and Tommy Tune have approached it. Most do not. Even when ideal conditions prevail, limited time and considerations of space inhibit the complete and exhaustive exploration of the dance possibilities inherent in the material—adding additional pressure to the mounting strains of preparing a major show. The job of all choreographers and dancers in a commercial venture is less a matter of delivering quality goods than of delivering quality goods in a limited amount of time. The highly stimulating and productive atmosphere of the inventive workshop format used first by Michael Bennett for *A Chorus Line* and, later, *Dreamgirls* personifies the ideal in creative and professional working conditions. Again, that option eludes all but successful, powerful few. Show business is a business, and its artists observe all the conventions of a profit-making enterprise.

Despite the time limitations and business pressures that circumscribe rehearsals, previews, or out-of-town tryouts, much has been achieved during two centuries of American show dancing. In place of standard routines whose aim is to stop the show, choreographers now offer sequences of dance images whose expression services the most fundamental needs of the theatrical event itself. In the best modern stage choreography, movement becomes the book in body language, with much of the music conceived and/or arranged to respond to the rhythms of the dances. Thus movement opens up to universal enjoyment entertainment that previously shut out everyone outside a specific language, tradition, or culture. The price to be paid? Better kinetic perception. Audiences content to regard dance only as a pleasant diversion now must be prepared to understand it as a vital means of communication. In retrospect, the emergence of movement as a dominant feature in entertainment packaging seems inevitable. The most vigorous American musical shows betrayed an allegiance to the physical and the visual in their determination to commit performance to the fullest possible use of the stage. To accomplish that, performers must move. When they move, that too can be choreographed. When a producer decrees that his musical must move, current choreographers interpret the word "move" to mean more than pace. Today's show moves when staging so externalizes concept or story in physical behavior that audiences must look to the "how" more than to the "what" to make sense of the evening's proceedings. Regrettable? Perhaps. But how very consistent with the modern American taste for style over substance.

Like the expansive and heralded cultural growth of the nation itself, American show dance reflects the melting-pot syndrome, in which vigorous cross-culturalization over a period of years ends with an offspring that has its own distinct identity. Ballet, modern dance, jazz, ethnic, ballroom, and disco each announce separate priorities, background, and clientele, yet American show dance embraces them all. Because our popular entertainments have always been sensitive to trends in public taste while simultaneously determining them, its tradition admits elements as diverse as the constituents of the American public itself. Unlike some other performing arts traditions that display unbroken continuity over decades, generations, perhaps even centuries, the American show dance tradition defines its character through diversity. Change? Presumed. Turnover? The rule. Unlike ballet, for instance, show dance has never had an institution like a national ballet company or, in the case of the United States, a series of major companies, committed to the preservation of the exact steps, style, and conventions of the major works of its heritage. Except for shreds of pictorial evidence in the clipping files of major research libraries, rare and poor-quality early films, and the recent efforts of the American Dance Machine, the dances of the American stage have been lost—victims of the rapid turnover typical of the business. Only the names of the steps, the stars, and the dances remain. Names like "hornpipe," "jig," "cakewalk," "buck and wing," "hootchy-kootchy," "waltz clog," "Charleston," "varsity Drag," "black bottom," "off to Buffalo," "lindy," "over the top," "through the trenches," "bump," "grind," "drag," "dip," "camel," "flick," "layout," "shimmy," and "grapevine" litter the show dance landscape of past and present as evidence of their continued use in original and redefined form as agents of kinetic effect, applause, or choreographic art.

While the evolution of the show dance tradition reflects a steady quantitative decline in the number of dancers employed for a single show (the early musical comedy dance director Seymour Felix assumed that a chorus of eighteen dancers constituted an *intimate* musical whereas today the number would be more like six), the quantitative decline stands in inverse proportion to the importance of the dance contribution itself. Considerable improvement in the training, versatility, and professional status of show dancers parallels that development. Where early-twentieth-century stage entertainments dramatized effort for applause, our best contemporary choreography conceals effort for valid artistic goals, and for that effort it rewards its makers and its doers with the status, fame, and riches consistent with show dancing's omnipresence on the American scene.

SHOW
DANCING
IN
AMERICA

1

The Earliest Show Dances

Although dramatic plays or plays with subsidiary song and dance dominated the repertory that touring companies offered American audiences in the eighteenth century, social dancing and what little theatrical dancing there was enjoyed considerable popularity during the crucial years of the American Revolution and the formative years of the federal republic. The heroes who fought the war and shaped the nation were also men who danced at balls and assemblies and, in order to improve their social stature, patronized the dance masters and schools of dance operated by the traveling performers. Although much dance instruction responded to an urgent need for cultivated social interaction in a colonial outpost adjacent to Indian territories, its presence served to educate the theatergoing population enough to applaud the similar if more accomplished efforts of professionals onstage.

The earliest American show dance mirrored the nature and customs of eighteenth-century England. That meant song-and-dance entertainment between the acts or such special added attractions as acrobatic feats, balancing acts, tumbling, or ropedancing—so advertised or not. It can be argued whether the motive for such curious, inappropriate, and yet customary behavior stemmed from the practical desire to conceal the unpleasant sounds of scenery being shifted or from a more genuine desire on the part of the touring company members to confront audiences as versatile performers "out of character." What is certain is that America's earliest audiences enjoyed exposure to such dance and movement diversions as the hornpipe, comic dances built around the Harlequin motif, tambourine dances, and a popular comic dance that came to be known by a variety of names such as the "drunken peasant," presumably because of the nature of the actions it depicted. Early management even

3

The contredanse was a corruption of the English "country dance," in which aristocratic dancers affected rustic attitudes and movement. (*Photo: Print and Picture Collection, Free Library of Philadelphia.*)

included Harlequin and Pierrot dance entertainment between the acts of John Gay's *The Beggar's Opera,* the eighteenth-century ballad opera whose amalgam of text, song, and dance set the form, tone, and standard of commercial success for early musical theater in America. Their repeated presence should not suggest that these dances were somehow supportive, related, or even virtuosic, but it does tell us that the early American playgoer took enough delight in stage dancing to convince wise managers to continue, if not expand, the practice. So lively was the public's interest in dancing that its inclusion as a special added attraction between the acts of Shakespearean productions was not uncommon. Individual dancing became the fashion at first, as when Master A. Hallam performed "A Punch's Dance." Then a slightly expanded treatment of dancing occurred when performers led others in a dance, as when James Godwin led the men of his company in a dance entitled "The Coopers." The inevitable extension of the practice took place when the entire cast assembled for group dances, such as one referred to as "A Country Dance" (usually a prototype of the reel). Each variation of single or combined dancing prevailed during the colonial and federal periods, thus establishing the prototypes for later stage dance: solo turns, female soloist with female chorus, male soloist with male chorus, and production number with the entire cast. Once group dancing became the fashion, the opportunity for spectacle became a reality that has never been abandoned on the American musical stage.

In its earliest phases, American stage entertainment followed the practice popular in contemporary England of featuring an afterpiece appended to the evening's entertainment and, as in England, the most popular and consistently offered afterpiece was the pantomime. Distant relatives of the commedia dell'arte reinterpreted by the English, the Harlequin pantomimes that became popular in colonial America adapted readily to national themes, famous heroes, patriotic incidents, or an occasional classical subject as frameworks for the exploits of the stock characters: Harlequin, his lover Columbine, her father Pantaloon, and the comic servant Clown. In the versions of this form staged in England by John Rich, pantomimes combined serious and comic elements by interpolating the comic adventures, tricks, and courtship antics of Harlequin and Columbine into breaks between the presentation of some serious narrative derived from a classical, folk, or contemporary source. Where contemporary drama relied on refinements of thought, language, and form, pantomimes favored the more theatrical effects to be achieved by scenery, costume, special effects, acrobatic display, and dance. Contemporary critics were known to attribute the appetite for such amusements to poor taste in their admirers. The pantomime developed for American audiences liberated the form from the conventions of its English antecedents, thus allowing for more topical commentary on serious and trivial issues of the day. Colonial and federal audiences favored two approaches to the pantomime: the nautical and the patriotic. Prominent examples carried titles like *Harlequin Shipwrecked; Shipwrecked Mariners Preserved; Fourth of July, or, The Sailor's Festival; American Independence;* and the *Battle of Trenton.* The English pantomime tradition inherited by colonial audiences featured diversified attractions assembled for the occasion. In 1785 a London performance of a pantomime entitled *Harlequin's Revenge* featured ropedancing, a "splendid display of machinery," eminent tumblers, two pantomime ballets, and a grand finale. The formula found its most appropriate expression in the early American circus, and some of the earliest feats of movement and dance recorded on the American entertainment scene are mentioned in conjunction with it. In 1794 a Philadelphia writer pointed out that among the performance accomplishments of the great equestrian John Bill Ricketts was the feat of dancing a hornpipe on a saddle as the horse galloped at full speed. As many in today's audience regard the Broadway musical as a vehicle for entertainment only, so did the late-eighteenth-century American audience regard the circus as popular amusement designed to relax and enliven. To that end managers bundled together into one highly popular show the contributions of tightrope dancers, slack-wire walkers, tumblers, clowns, equestrian feats, balancing acts, pantomimes, singing, dancing, and fireworks. Movement, it is clear, figured prominently in the overall entertainment package. Now as then, successful performance demanded skills associated with dance: physical control, discipline, agility, balance, and acrobatic talent. The means were the same, only the ends were different. In 1795 the Old America Company postponed the performance of a play rather than compete with the circus. The contemporary historian William Dunlap wrote, "*School for Scandal* gave way for Ricketts and Clown." No doubt, audiences received a considerable return for their investment in a ticket. Prices ranged from one dollar for a box to a half-dollar for the pit. So profitable was the enterprise that when Ricketts's Troupe opened at the New York Amphitheatre on September 15, 1795, management funded all alterations of the place to accommodate the scenery, props, machinery, and "decoration."

A more sophisticated use of movement took place in the pantomime-ballets that offered dramatic action without speech (but with stylized gesture) to musical accompaniment. The pantomime-ballets relied on stage movement to establish character, portray situation, and develop plot. Traditionally, the form used two types of mime: (1) the artificial or symbolic gesture accepted by the audience as a convention, and (2) the expressive gesture derived from real life and recognized by the audience as such. The text of a serious pantomime in three acts entitled *La Forêt Noire, or, Maternal Affection* that Madame Gardie performed at the Boston Theatre to "merited applause" confirms that production's dependence on the latter. The first six scenes of Act I are reprinted here, courtesy of the University of Pennsylvania. Scholars acknowledge the script to be the earliest extant of any pantomime performed on the early American stage.

ACT I

SCENE I

The Theatre represents an antique Saloon. The back scene, or bottom, has, on one side the Portrait of an Officer, hidden by another picture representing a Landscape; on the other side a low Window, which opens. On the left of the scene a Library or Book-Case; a little further a Table, with a drawer; on the other side a Forte Piano.

Lucille enters, holding in her hand the basket, in which is the breakfast of her child; she sits it down on the table, goes near the book-case and listens; not hearing any noise she presumes that her child sleeps yet; she sits down a moment, shewing the greatest disquiet; she attempts to work, but appears distracted, having her attention and looks fixed upon the book-case, to seize the moment of the child's waking, to give him his breakfast; she looks often at the portrait which is at the bottom or flat scene, and sighs. She rises, goes near the portrait, and is going to uncover it; stops, and goes to see if she may not be surprised by any one, returns to the picture, and uncovering it, discovers the portrait of her lover. She traverses the Theatre, showing the picture of her lover, and her love for him; she looks by turns at the portrait, the book-case and the chamber of her father—shews her tenderness for her child, and the chagrin which she feels from the ignorance in which her father is, of her situation; the sight of the portrait affects her so much, that she cannot resist her desire to see the child. She assures herself anew that she cannot be surprised, goes to the forte, strikes the keys, which is the signal for the child, who answers by playing an air upon his flagelet. She opens the book-case.

SCENE II

(Lucille and Adolphus)

The child comes out, embraces his mother, asks to see the picture of his father; she refuses; he throws himself on his knees, and caresses her anew; she cannot refuse him and *discovers the picture*; the child shews the greatest joy in seeing it, he tries to embrace it, but not being tall enough he sends it kisses, returns to his mother and embraces her. A noise is heard, *Lucille* frightened, gives the basket to the child, and shuts him up; she covers the picture, and seats herself near the forte. Hearing nothing, she rises and goes to the door—returning, she sees her lover at the window.

SCENE III

Lucille, after looking at him some time in doubt, throws herself into his arms. They show the greatest joy. He asks where his child is; she answers that he is in the same room; he searches, she sits down near the forte, and laughs at his embarrassment. He returns to her, and begs her to tell him where the child is. *Lucille* strikes the forte, the child answers with his flagelet. The officer listens, but cannot discover from whence the sound comes; he insists anew, that she would tell him where the child is. *Lucille* leads him to the book-case—the moment that she is going to show him the secret way to open it, some one knocks. *Lucille* presses her lover to go out; he insists on first seeing his child. She supplicates, he consents. *Lucille,* in great terror, accompanies him to the window; she bids him adieu, sees him descend, shuts the window, and returns to the front of the stage.

SCENE IV
(*Lucille, Geronte and L'Abbé*)

The father enters with the *Abbe. Lucille* meets her father, and kisses his hand. The *Abbe* looks at her through his glass. She regards him with disdain. The father presents the *Abbe,* ordering her to receive him for her husband. *Lucille* is much distressed. Her father urges her; she refuses. (*Exit the father in a rage.*)

SCENE V
(*Lucille and Abbe*)

She looks at him with disdain; he attempts to make his court; she turns her back. He offers her his *bouquet*; she refuses. He offers her some cakes; she refuses. He consoles himself by eating some of them; he takes his snuff-box, and offers snuff. *Lucille* vexed, strikes it out of his hand. He menaces to tell her father, and *Exit in a rage.*

SCENE VI
(*Lucille*)

She sits a moment, appears to reflect; shows her fears that her father will force her to marry the *Abbe,* and falls in despair, upon the forte.

Mime makes narrative ballet possible, and the early American merchants of the pantomime-ballet were quick to adapt existing dramatic and ballad opera material to theater pieces told in the language of movement. For instance, George Washington's favorite ballad opera (one of the most widely performed stage entertainments in America before 1800) was entitled *The Poor Soldier* and was converted into the pantomime-ballet *Dermot and Kathleen.* The spin-off proved so successful that it received as many Philadelphia performances as did its model during the closing years of the eighteenth century.

The success of the pantomime-ballet led the way to American audience acceptance of the nineteenth-century Romantic ballet and the subsequent adulation for a parade of European dancers who toured the United States with specimens from its repertoire. The critical and commercially successful tours of Fanny Elssler and Marie and Phillipe Taglioni fixed the Romantic ballet firmly and forever in the affection of American audiences.

The term "Romantic ballet" implies both a period and a style.

Historically, it mirrored the cultural imperatives of the Romantic movement that swept the literature, painting, and music of Europe and America into open revolt against the ideals of neoclassicism that dominated the arts during the preceding century. Where eighteenth-century artists labored to achieve balance, decorum, restraint, polish, and self-effacing objectivity, Romantics valued passion, power, individuality, and originality. Out went the themes and characters of classical mythology; in marched material drawn from tales, legends, and fairy and folk tales. This was the period during which the ballerina rose to her toes for the first time—a movement made famous after Taglioni's appearance in the first great Romantic ballet, *La Sylphide*—and the event brought an ethereal, floating otherworldly quality to the dance that has personified the Romantic style ever since.

American show dance has never been without its stars. Wildly fluctuating levels of talent and training aside, advertising and publicity considerations demand that management capitalize on the name, reputation, and notoriety of the product about to be shown to the public for profit. The first American show dance star and our first professional native-born actor was John Durang (1768–1822), billed in all modesty as "the greatest dancer in America." When John Durang played in provincial cities like Harrisburg, Pennsylvania, he charged fifty cents for a box seat and twenty-five cents for the gallery and pulled in crowded houses every night. Durang tried to do everything: Shakespeare, acrobatics, puppet shows, horsemanship, fireworks, circus routines, pantomimes, comedy, dancing, building playhouses, and constructing scenery. Most contemporary critics panned John Durang as an actor, claiming that he played even the most minor roles badly. They must have been right, for throughout his career the type of role that invariably came his way was that of an Indian, a Moor, or an aborigine—parts that required very little speech or dramatic complexity at that time. Paradoxically, Durang's limitations assured him a place in American theatrical history as one of the first burnt-cork specialists on the entertainment scene. The time: December 5, 1792. The role: Robinson Crusoe's Man Friday. The play: a pantomime based on Daniel Defoe's *Robinson Crusoe*. For such an ambitious career, Durang's only formal training came as apprentice to a dancing master from whom he learned specific dances, technique, and an appreciation of dance music and costuming. The combination of training and talent made him the unchallenged hornpipe specialist of early American show business. The hornpipe is a step dance thought to have originated in the English countryside and associated (some claim incorrectly) with sailors because the descriptive movements of the arms in some variations suggest life at sea and the performance of shipboard tasks, as does the rolling, side-to-side movement. Since theatrical versions of the dance became a popular staple of the "additional entertainments" between acts or scenes of legitimate stage offerings, most touring companies featured someone who could dance it. James Godwin of the Old America Company danced it. Henrietta Osborne danced it in "revealing" male clothing as if in anticipation of the late-nineteenth-century burlesque performances by women dressed as men in form-revealing tights. Nevertheless, it was John Durang who danced it best, probably because it was a favorite with him. His autobiography, *The Memoir of John Durang,* offers a primary source of insight into the training, artistic concerns, and development of the show-dancing component of his career. As well as hornpipes, Durang executed highland flings, allemandes, waltzes, minuets, and reels, in addition to the standard show business fare of acrobatics, tumbling, vaulting, and ropedancing. His repertory of steps included the "pigeon wing," the "shuffle," and the "heel-and-toe haul." Even more reassuring was an artistic concern for correct style, an understanding of what he called the "anatomy" of a step, and—as is the case with great dancers who became great teachers—an ability to make his students master his steps and dances.

Of more importance to the evolution of show dances created in the United States was the arrival of the colorful French dancer, acrobat, and choreographer Alexandre Placide. In addition to exhibitions of "manly feats" on the tightrope, Placide created numerous pastoral pantomime-ballets—a practice that assured a consistent flow of seemingly new and different works to accommodate box-office demand. Wrote a contemporary critic in an article entitled, "The Charleston Stage Sixty Years Ago":

> The first time I ever saw him was at Charleston, S.C., about 1801 dancing the tight-rope. At that period, it was considered a great and graceful feat of address, and always drew crowded houses . . . The preparations for the dance were always imposing. The attendants in livery, carried the rope to the center of the pit, where it was duly attached and drawn upon the stage. A palace scene was set for the rope dancing, and a row of wax candles were placed at equal distances near the rope. Placide, habited in light silk Spanish dress with silk stockings and pumps and two watch chains, then greatly in fashion, made his appearance amid shouts of applause. . . .

As a choreographer and manager, Placide believed in female beauty as the surest guarantee of commercial success. The *New York Clipper* quoted him on the subject. "Give me . . . de pretty vimmens; I don't care, den, for de talent." Unlike John Durang, who was mostly self-trained in the skills that supported his career, French ballet performers like Placide were products of a rigid and formal system, the *danse d'école* of the Royal Academy of Dance. The impact of their presence impressed on American audiences more exacting standards of dance construction and performance than had been seen on the early American stage. Certainly the foreign dancers attracted to colonial America did not represent the best Europe had to offer. A nation in its infancy could hardly offer the type of audience or a suitable market for highbrow Parisian dance fare. Yet, our shores did attract some brave and hardy dancers eager to escape European political instability, dancers whose attempts at ballet theater—however provincial—would later make possible a succession of visits from European superstars like the Taglionis, Marius Petipa, and, most notably, Fanny Elssler.

The Fanny Elssler tour began in 1840 and ran for two years of ecstatic reviews and boffo box office. Her New York debut at the Park Theatre sold out for the entire two-week engagement, assuring the star a reported $7,000 profit. The frenzy and adoration about foreign ballet stars in America—which in our time centered around the artistic defections of Rudolf Nureyev, Natalia Makarova, and Mikhail Baryshnikov—began over a century ago with the frenzied tribute accorded Fanny Elssler. Young men pulled her carriage through the streets of New York. Theater management in Baltimore auctioned tickets for her performances to the highest bidders. In Washington, D.C., the Congress of the United States adjourned so that its members could attend her performances. But her visit was a triumph of celebrity, nothing more, leaving no indelible aesthetic mark. When Elssler returned triumphantly to Europe, she left nineteenth-century American dance as she found it—poised somewhere between hornpipes, tightrope exhibitions, and vulgar entertainments on the one hand and the decidedly foreign "fancy dancing" of pantomime and Romantic ballet on the other. Not until the American musical stage began to draw inspiration and material from indigenous sources rather than imported entertainment from across the Atlantic did American show dance acquire a distinctly American flavor—and a future.

2

The Black
Dance Tradition
and Minstrelsy

The European dance forms that dominated the musical stage of colonial and federal America yielded to a less refined but more vigorous and popular dancing wrought from the real and imagined heritage of the Afro-American slave during the period of minstrelsy and thereafter. With the first slave ships that deposited live African cargo on American shores early in the seventeenth century came a potent dance force composed of the movement customs of many tribes forced together by the political power of the white race into the social, cultural, and serviceable commodity that came to be known as slavery. During that shameful period, a century before the concept became socially fashionable and politically respectable, many were cast into the American melting pot, except that our first unwilling immigrants represented the tribes of Africa bound for servitude in a new land and not the various nationalities of Western Europe that flocked to the New World in search of wealth, fame, and a better life. On plantations and on the streets of New York, slave and city blacks danced to the accompaniment of chants and drums, rivaling each other in dances for pride or profit, and so begat a dance tradition whose elements are visible still on Broadway, film, and video.

The black dance that evolved in America as a means of racial survival and later as a form of private and public entertainment derived from an African heritage of movement as religious and emotional affirmation. The African committed the body in motion to the gods and spirits of the forest and plain. At festivals and ceremonies, at burials and coming-of-age rituals, movements of the feet and hands and head and torso together revealed the joy or grief of the moment. Far from the blur of wild, wanton, and disorganized flailing about depicted in so many terrible Hollywood movies, African dances embrace recognizable forms

12

The characteristic use of movement in a circle can be seen in this African children's torch dance, Niger, about 1893. (*Photo: Print and Picture Collection, Free Library of Philadelphia*)

that allow participants subtle variations in movement and expression. Regional and tribal differences account for broad stylistic variations. Scholars trace movement directed from the hips and pelvis to the tribes of the Congo, predominant head and upper torso activity to the West African coastal area of Dahomey, and vigorous footwork to the Pygmy tribes of the African rain forests. Whatever the regional characteristics, all move to the beat of the drum. Specific dances might feature one or more couples engaged in a forward-and-backward shuffle surrounded by a circle of singing, clapping participants. Generally, African dance utilizes the entire body, with the pulsating torso as base and center for movement and bodily extension. Usually the pelvis and hips stand out as the source of movement, with hands and legs relegated to secondary importance. An eyewitness account of early-eighteenth-century dances of the Nigerian coast attests to characteristics that surface later in the black

dances of U.S. and West Indian plantations. Those characteristics are:
(1) a recurrence of movement in a circle or dances in the round; (2) foot
movement, such as beating the feet on the ground as an extension of the
movement originated in the hip and pelvic area; and (3) frequent forward
projections of the pelvis that appear to suggest the rhythm and motion
of the sexual act.

Mainly, African dances moved on the beat as a natural response of
the entire body to the beat of the drum. Dances executed in unison aimed
for direct correlation between the accent of the drumbeat and the earth-
stomping beating of the feet, a compliance sometimes relieved by the
subtle variation of perfectly timed pauses also executed in unison. The
drumbeat followed the dancers into slavery as they stomped in their
shackles and danced in their chains on slave ships destined for the
plantations of the Old South. The dances of Africa didn't die in the
socially inhospitable climate of the New World but adapted to the needs
of the dancers to survive, please their owners, or entertain the landed
gentry at public plantation entertainments. Soon, popular musical entertainments based on sentimental appraisals of plantation life from the
white viewpoint swept the nation, on their way to becoming the most
popular form of entertainment in the United States during the middle
decades of the nineteenth century. The form's most visible and successful
performers looked to the hybrid Afro-American dance tradition for
inspiration, steps, and the altogether indigenous qualities that set it
apart from the show dance derived from European models. On the
considerable journey from authentic African dance transplanted to the
American plantations of the antebellum South, to the metamorphosis of
black dance elements into tap, jazz, Broadway dancing, and disco,
American show dance paused at a critical juncture. They called it
minstrelsy.

American minstrelsy was a simple, unsophisticated form of song,
dance, and comedy entertainment that dominated the public entertainment scene until the advent of vaudeville, burlesque, and extravaganza.
Its potency as show business derived from managerial commitment to
offer inexpensive, accessible shows housed in "elegantly appointed,"
conveniently located theaters. A February 29, 1880, *Boston Sunday Globe*
account of the opening of Hooley's Theatre catalogued the attraction of
a form of musical entertainment four dacades old and vigorous still:

The beautiful Novelty Theatre, whose earliest prospects were blighted by
bad management, now comes to the front again. This time it is under the

direction of a man whose name inspires confidence and almost assures success in advance—Uncle Dick Hooley. One of the oldest and most popular of America's caterers to public amusement, Mr. Hooley is certain to maintain in Boston the reputation he has so honorably gained throughout the country. A gem of a house is the theatre of which he assumes control—appointed elegantly in every way, and possessing peculiar advantages as to location. Situated as it is at the corner of Dover and Washington streets, it is very nearly in the centre of the city, close to the great South End district, and within three minutes' walk of South Boston, with its population of 60,000. Arrangements have been made with the street-car and omnibus lines for the convenience of patrons; and Hooley's Theatre may already be counted a popular resort. As a home of refined minstrelsy the house will fill a vacant place, and those who remember the palmy days of Morris Brothers, Pell Trowbridge and Buckley's Serenaders, will be the first to welcome the famous

EMERSON'S MEGATHERIAN MINSTRELS

who are to give the opening entertainment at Hooley's this coming week. It is a strong company indeed, and just such a one as Manager Hooley might be expected to offer. There is Billy Emerson, the very popular comedian, and one of the most artistic song-and-dance men in the country. . . . The prices of admission have been placed at very moderate figures—25, 35, 50 and 75 cents. Performances will be given each evening, and on Wednesday and Saturday afternoons. Reserved seats are now ready.

The source of minstrel show material was the soil of the Old South. The romantic image of plantation slaves with their comic antics, crooning melodies, and shuffling dances provided the model upon which performers, shows, and specialty acts patterned their material. Accompanied as they were by banjos, tambourines, and bone clappers, blackface minstrel songs provided splendid aural incentive for lively dance. Within the framework of the minstrel show's full evening of entertainment—originated by the Virginia Minstrels in 1843 and perfected by the Christy Minstrels, among others—dancers discovered the broadest possible range of opportunities for exploiting the movement heritage of the black slave. When transformed imaginatively for entertainment purposes, these dancers brought about a demand for dance as a show's integral attraction, not merely its accompaniment. Contemporary accounts acknowledge that it was the quality and notoriety of its dance appeal that assured the popular success of minstrel troupes like Charles White's Kitchen Minstrels, generally regarded as the best of the kind on the Civil

War era minstrelsy circuit. At the height of their popularity, the Al. G. Field Greater Minstrel Co. advertised a show entitled *When the Moonlight Falls and the Water Ripples* as a "mammoth Singing and Dancing Divertisement," the "Greatest Minstrel Presentation of the Age." The following advertisement is an example of those used to entice audiences, and its makeup attests to the vital contribution dancers made to the internal workings of the show as well as the external need for advertisement and publicity:

> The scene is one of a tropical woodland in the evening. The moon steals over a low range of the hill and its light shows a party of white ladies and gentlemen in a boat which is floating down the current of a river in the distance. The darkies gather and indulge in their moonlight songs and dances, the white folks replying to their melody. The scene is closed by the darkies singing to the birds of the forest, and one of their number—a yodler—follows the song of the mockingbird while his companions listen for the echo to steal back through the forest. There is a quick change, and when the lights go up it is noon on the lawn in front of a Southern home. The darkies come in from the fields singing one of the old melodies and dance their buck and wing steps. These dances never fail to make a hit, and the harmony that lies within the soul of the darkies is developed and expressed in the rhythm of their feet. With the Al. G. Field Greater Minstrels this season is a corps of dancers who are as expert as any who can be found in America.

Another Al. G. Field Greater Minstrels production, entitled *Roll On Silvery Moon,* promised an entertainment extravaganza to which dancing would make a substantial contribution:

> The moon is the subject of the big spectacular and musical extravaganza presented by the Al. G. Field Greater Minstrels. Yon peeping moon sees the old world at a time when human eyes are not as penetrating as at noon-day. Sights and scenes familiar and strange are depicted in the mimetic stage review that will excite the risibilities of a stoic. Life after dark is always an interesting study. Nothing more beautiful and realistic in stage illustrations was ever produced than this series of stirring scenes.
>
> Interspersed with musical numbers embracing all the salient features of comic opera, burlesque and musical comedy. Gorgeous costuming, brilliant effects, the intricate dances originated by Doc Quigley for this dazzling, dancing divertisement. The great variety of business, the character impersonations, the enchanting vocal numbers are all of a character that imprints on this big production the stamp of greatness. Yon peeping moon will bring

to mind and memory many amusing incidents in life, long forgotten, and introduce new thoughts that will make pleasant recollections hereafter.

The Poetry of Motion as exemplified by the Dexterous dancers who comprise a round two dozen or more of the big company, the Al. G. Field Minstrels, are under the limelight or the moonlight during a greater part of the program. The spectacle, "Roll on, Silvery Moon," was expressly devised to exploit the cleverness of the dancing contingent.

Among the many dancers are:

Doc Quigley	Jack Sully
Bun Granville	Tommy Odell
Frank Miller	Louis Tracy
Joe Egan	Fred Raycroft
Pat Hughes	P. J. Scanlon
Shelvey Bros.	Jules Hanlon
Thomas Callahan	Will C. Long
Chas. Caldwell	Henry Gibbons
Frank Tracy	Meyer Sardell
Sylvester Reardon	

The showmen who contributed most to the rise of American minstrelsy recognized the importance of the dance component from the start. When blackface performers first began to band together in the 1840s to form minstrel show troupes, one of the most prominent talent combinations was that of banjoist and dancer. Since the most successful troupes toured extensively, their dancing received exposure in the British Isles and elsewhere. Advance publicity promised the audience as much dance as comedy and song. When Dan Emmett and the Virginia Minstrels toured Scotland as "the first band of minstrels ever organized," the theater presented their show in conjunction with a comedy performed by its own dramatic company. Through the medium of "songs, dances, lectures, refrains, sayings and doings," the Virginia Minstrels promised to portray "the oddities, pecularities, eccentricities, whimsicalities and comicalities of that sable genus of humanity." Included on the program were dances "such as slaves dance on their holiday feasts and in gathering-in the cotton and sugar crops, entitled 'Corn Husking Jig and Marriage Festival Dance.'" Broadsides assured the public that "not a trace or shade of vulgarity is mixed in . . ." and that "there is nothing that can offend in the least degree the most fastidious taste." The program for the following day's performance promised that a Mr. R. W. Pelham of the Virginia Minstrels, the "neatest and best dancer living," would appear in several of his new songs and dances. In addition, Mr. Dan Emmett's celebrated banjo variations would accompany Mr. Pelham ". . . who will show de science ob de heel to de music ob de banjo, making a grand display ob de heel-and-toe caperbilities . . . when de right leg, de leff leg, de hind leg, and ole de odder legs will be brought to bear on dat 'ticular 'casion." As the language suggests, minstrel showmen built their comedy on stage caricatures of American blacks, of whom the two principal examples were the shiftless, uncouth clown and the "ludicrous" blackface personification of the white dandy. Both characters adapted successfully to dance. After the Civil War, when black minstrel troupes inherited the same duo, the dandy strutted and the clown shuffled. Minstrel-show dance settled on a hybrid, derivative style, based on Northern white idealized or comic interpretations of plantation life, whose animation, vigor, and robust theatricality appeared to contemporary audiences to be more authentic, at least more appropriate to a show's subject matter, than the songs, their lyrics, the jokes, or the burlesque. Eventually, there arose a body of steps and dances as well as a style; it would sustain a century of American show dance through vaudeville, revue, nightclub acts, and early musical comedy. It is during the minstrelsy era that we first encounter the names by which steps and dances still evident in the modern repertory came to be known, and the earliest descriptions of the dancers themselves, which together constitute the earliest substantive historical record of show dance for the American public.

Without a doubt, the most ubiquitous, functional, and creatively subscribed minstrel dance was the walkaround, a promenade dance that often concluded the first part of a show. Initially a soloist performed the dance, but time and popularity saw it grow into an ensemble number for a small group of dancers, the entire company, or both. Dan Emmett wrote "Dixie" not as a Civil War anthem but as a walkaround for the Bryant's Minstrels. The walkaround demands suitable music, usually a lively tune in 2/4 time. The writers and performers of minstrelsy conceived the walkaround as a finale to one part of the show, with the often-exercised option to reprise for the finale of the entire production. To the pronounced rhythm of march time, and with steps based on variations of leg elevations with the body in layback position, an entire company could engulf the stage in a vigorous kinetic spectacle that would bring down the curtain and provoke rousing applause. The format of the walkaround permitted the inclusion of challenge dances designed to involve the audience in the spirit of the good-natured competition between dancers or groups of dancers on the stage. The cakewalk evolved from just such a challenge-dance situation. In its earliest form, the cakewalk was a contest among dancing couples who attempted to outdo each other in the mock imitation of the white man's manners and behavior. Popular consensus determined the best couple, whose prize was a lavishly decorated cake. The practice originated the expression "to take the cake," and the dance itself appended the name "cakewalk." A contemporary pamphlet entitled *Negro Minstrels: Jokes, Gags, Speeches* offers the would-be minstrel some tips on packaging and performing the cakewalk:

Cake walks have become such a popular craze during the last few years that society everywhere are introducing them in their many social events, and minstrel performances now seem incomplete without them. While it is a difficult matter to explain everything connected with the many movements, etc., in a cake walk, the author has used his best endeavors to make it plain to the reader. In the first place, to successfully take part in a cake walk, each participant should take great pains in your make-up. The most extreme and flashy suits should be worn, including an endless variety of diamonds or Rhine stones, for jewelry effects. The young lady or young man that takes such part should wear bright colored dresses. Large hat and high heel slippers and carry parasol or fan which will show off in excellent taste. The gentleman partner should wear a Prince Albert coat made of red, blue, brown or green satin, high silk hat of same material, checked trousers, patent leather shoes with white gaiters, a cane with crooked handle, decorated with ribbons of same colors as his lady's dress. Where more than one couple take part, try and have your costumes, both ladies and gentlemen, different from one another.

Start your walk by taking partner's hand, elevating it to about the height of your head; step off somewhat in advance of lady, assuming a happy smile; keep step with each time of the music, and be sure to step only on ball of foot, letting the heel down gently as you touch the other foot to the floor. After passing the audience once in that position let go of hands and continue to walk alone, meeting again at front of audience with bow. Lady will then take your arm and continue walk halfway round when she discovers her shoe untied. You will then proceed with much grace and a bow. Kneeling, place your handkerchief upon knee, and placing lady's foot thereon, proceed to tie it, after which he will arise and accept a kiss which she will offer. The most essential point in a cake walk is to always keep your face towards the audience, not matter if walking directly away from them with your backs turned.

Put in your walks as much different steps or figures as possible, such as imitating an old colored man, a Hebrew, a German, etc., and always bear in mind that the hands, arms and face have as much to do with your success as the walking part. A graceful swing of the arms, or if carried out away from the body, is always clever.

The dances of the specialty acts that formed the second part of most minstrel shows represented a miscellany of jigs, clogs, hornpipes, and dances separately classified as fancy, comic, and grotesque. The San Francisco Minstrels featured double clog exercises and a "grand corn husking dance." The program for the second part of Huntley's Minstrels announced an Ethiopian jig, a challenge dance, and a burlesque fancy dance. Minstrel dancing may have borrowed style and substance from the plantation, but much of its form and many of its steps came from the theatrical use of clog dancing and the Irish jig. Clog dancing took its name from the heavy shoes (usually with wooden soles) that dancers wore to beat out the rhythms of the dance. A clog dance is a *sounded* dance. Performance characteristics include an erect body posture and passive facial expressions put to the service of stomping out an amazing number of sounds per measure of music. On the other hand, the jig was a fast, happy, and bouncing dance executed with erect posture to music in triple time. Because the Afro-American step dances favored flat-footed steps directed to the ground with bare feet, the minstrel dance hybrid added the qualities of dragging, gliding, and shuffling to the older percussive style of jig and clog. Minstrel dancing embraced influences from the Old World and the New, with each innovative performer adding the ideas, approaches, and techniques that guaranteed personal success in a highly competitive field and assured the longevity of the dancing itself. Like so much early show dance in America, minstrelsy glorified steps—not expression, virtuosity, movement, imagery, or storytelling—but steps. The steps that embraced most of what was Afro-American in the hybrid dance tradition of minstrelsy were called the "essence of Old Virginia" and the buck-and-wing. The former was a gliding step achieved by subtle heel-and-toe movement that propelled the dancer across the stage to music in slow tempo. The lowest reaches of the feet held the secret to correct performance, not the position and force generated by the legs, as in jigs and clogs. Less famous in their time, but more visible in later manifestations of American show dance, were the steps collectively referred to as the buck-and-wing. Although explanations vary widely, there is good reason to believe that the buck step was originally a vain and extroverted strut built on the contrasting impulses of swaggering gait and relaxation, while the wing was a horizontally executed air step descended from the "pigeon wing" of the plantation—a dance described by a contemporary source in images relating the practice of clipping pigeons' wings to the dancer flapping arms and legs to the side, much as the unfortunate bird might do.

At the height of the form's popularity, all major minstrel troupes featured one or more dance specialists who were advertised in superlatives despite their generally acknowledged lack of formal dance training. When Huntley's Minstrels appeared at Sanford's Opera House in Philadelphia, they paraded the virtues of Mert Sexton, "the Greatest Comic Dancer of the Present Era, whose Wonderful Eccentricities has heralded his name throughout the country. . . ." The Morris Bros., Pell and Trowbridge's Minstrels toured "13 Star Performers" with top billing accorded Dick Sliter, "the Champion Dancer" who performed "A Fancy Hornpipe" and "A Champion Jig." In addition, management engaged talented boy dancers for the sentimental, surefire effects children have always been able to achieve on the professional stage. When the leading troupe of its time, the George Christy's Minstrels, appeared at New York's Niblo's Saloon in 1859, it featured a Master Gus Howard, "pupil of George Christy" and "the youngest Jig Dancer, Tambourinest and Bone Player Living." Rumsey and Newcomb's Original Campbell Minstrels presented "the Grotesque and Fancy Dancer Master Eddy (Late of the Ronzani Ballet Troupe) who performed an Ethiopian Fling." What could the San Francisco Minstrels do under the circumstances but call the attention of the public to *their* "Champion Dancer of the World: Master Jerry"?

When a reporter asked the old-time minstrel Hughey Dougherty about his early decision to become a burnt-cork showman, he replied,

> How did I get into the business? Well, I used to be a printer's devil, that's how I started in life . . . but I got to dancing jigs and I thought more about the jigs than I did about my work. . . . I kept up the jig dancing and learned funny songs and everybody said I ought to go into the minstrel business. . . .

Nevertheless, minstrelsy rewarded its best dancers with major careers on the American stage, first in minstrelsy itself and later in the minstrel acts of vaudeville. Even the competition acknowledged that "the beautiful dancer and elegant singer" Billy Emerson was "one of the most graceful men on the stage." Ralph Keeler built a reputation on his "Lucy Long," a sand dance in the early shuffling style that later specialists would develop into the soft shoe of vaudeville and musical comedy. Billy Kersands achieved fame as the master of the "essence of Old Virginia," during which he so maneuvered his 200 pounds as to glide in airy suspension across the floor. And the graceful, elegant George Primrose danced the best soft shoe on the American stage for decades.

If virtuosic dancing can be said to secure the reputation of what is danced, then no dancer did more for nineteenth-century show dance than William Henry Lane, the legendary Master Juba. Born a free black in Virginia around 1825, Master Juba's talent and prodigy so propelled him to the forefront of American stage performers that by the time he reached twenty, the most discriminating critics and peers acknowledged him as "the very greatest of dancers." In fact, his fame and theatrical prestige were so considerable that in 1845 he toured pre–Civil War America with four white minstrels and received top billing. Master Juba wasn't a specialist so much as a multitalented theatrical personality—like so many of the best "gypsies" on the modern Broadway stage. His audiences at home and abroad recognized unanimously the gifts of a first-rate singer, tambourine virtuoso, and "the best jig dancer of the era." Great dancers are great at an early age, and Master Juba was a precocious phenomenon even for his time. It was said that he danced as naturally as he breathed, with the always artistically sound properties of effortless execution, unsurpassed grace, and uncommon endurance. He was black, yet he felt no obligation to offer the public the authentic dances of his Afro-American heritage. His business was show business, and his commitment was to the inherited conventions of stage performance that enveloped his professional life. Since a contemporary critic compared his dancing to the pluck and percussion sounds of banjo and bones, we can infer that his appeal resembled that of later dancers in the tap dance tradition, whose aural presence as a musical instrument distinguished their technique and the effects it achieved.

Although minstrelsy disappeared from the American scene, its dance contributions are still carried on by dance studios, choreographers, and popular performers. Just as the three separate acts of the minstrel-show format evolved into vaudeville, revue, and burlesque, so too would minstrel dance steps and styles continue in fanciful reincarnations on the popular stage and in the social dance of the American public. The Charleston craze of the 1920s incorporated the variation of the Juba dance involving the crossing and uncrossing of the hands back and forth across the knees. Bob Fosse's staging of *Pippin* involved minstrelsy motifs, particularly in the number "War Is a Science." When the famous minstrel dancer Eddie Leonard was asked whether his crossover from minstrelsy to early musical comedy involved flying to a different branch of the amusement tree or merely perching on a different twig requiring comparable ability, he replied:

> . . . musical comedy technique is not so different from that of minstrelsy, and . . . the dancing which will set to tapping the toes of a minstrel show audience will also start a syncopation wave among the musical comedy crowd. The old time buck dancing and also the soft-shoe steps which I am using . . . are remnants of the minstrels days of Billy Emerson and I have lifted them bodily into musical comedy with very little change.

The show dance of the American stage absorbs its predecessors gently and by degrees.

3

Dance Specialties During the Vaudeville Era

Vaudeville's ascendancy to America's premier form of entertainment during the decades that preceded and followed the turn of the century paralleled the extension and development of American show dance and added to the fund of rhythmic jig and clog dances the decidedly new and different strains of ballroom, ethnic, and toe dancing and an energetic tap dancing that would come to dominate the musical entertainments of Broadway and Hollywood. The career of that "Grand Old Man of Minstrelsy—Eddie Leonard" spanned that phase of American show business. To many, he represented the lone practitioner, in the newer medium of vaudeville, of an old style of show dancing—the sand-dancing, soft-shoe, clog, and step tradition epitomized by George Primrose in minstrelsy. Yet, when Leonard and his company of singers and dancers headlined the B. F. Keith Theatre vaudeville bill, the act felt obliged to include "the most up to date" trends in dance as well. Eddie Leonard recognized that despite the allegiance of older members of the audience to the old style, new dancing and types of dancers needed to be acknowledged during this period of expansion and transition for popular show dance. Variety acts nourished the system that was vaudeville, and the variety of dance acts on the circuit attest to the diversity, vigor, and popularity of dance entertainment during this period.

Why make vaudeville the focus of this phenomenon? More than any other entertainment alternative in its time Vaudeville encouraged, if not precipitated, the quantitative and varietal expansion of dance acts before the public. Most vaudeville circuits included at least one song-and-dance act or minimusical revue on the bill. The system valued uniqueness and encouraged diversity. Some dancers traded on talent or technique; others developed unusual material. There were Dutch dancers, Russian dancers,

Irish dancers, blackface minstrel dancers, whiteface minstrel dancers, flash acts, class acts, toe dancers, knockabouts, acrobatic dancers, competition acts, and legomania. Even the celebrated originators of modern dance—Martha Graham, Doris Humphrey, and Charles Weidman—did their stints in vaudeville. What a hotbed of dance activity the vaudeville stage must have been during the height of its popularity between 1890 and 1920! It served as a professional school, a training ground, and an experimental station for the dancers destined for Broadway, nightclubs, and film and as a well-paying alternative between more lucrative engagements. Producers from every form of musical entertainment raided vaudeville for dancers. To interpolate a sole specialty dancer or a knockout specialty act into a book show, revue, or screenplay presented no artistic problems to management, particularly if the dancer or the act was already famous. Vaudeville troupers really worked for their fame. Without today's electronic media that make performers familiar to millions of viewers in minutes, the dance acts of the vaudeville era earned their exposure on the road. Vaudeville circuits crisscrossed the length and breadth of the United States, bringing live entertainment to a considerable public at a very low price. Even when a famous vaudeville dance act moved on to Broadway or Hollywood, no attempt was made to adapt performer or performance to the new medium. It was the custom to make the dancer or the act solely responsible for its own dance material. Not a bad idea for its time; invariably, the vaudevillian knew what to do. A successful vaudeville dance act had to be masterfully paced; graced with an imaginative or at least interesting entrance; a rousing, applause-assured exit; and no dead time in between. When the curtain rose in vaudeville, the act was on its own. You knew what to do or you learned. You learned what to do or you left.

A look at the inventory of vaudeville dance specialties reveals several not-altogether-exclusive categories that collectively represent the major areas of concentration: eccentric dancing, comic dancing, acrobatic dancing (including legomania), step or tap dancing, and toe dancing. Difficulties that issue from widespread disagreement over definition, terminology, and interpretation inhibit any unequivocal approach to the dance discipline of the vaudeville era. Dancers then as now brought a unique body, a special way of moving, and highly individual attitudes and approaches to their own dancing and to their regard for the dancing of others. Unlike dancers, the musical entertainment artists who create librettos, music, lyrics, orchestrations, and set and costume designs leave some tangible, physical artifact that gives concrete testimony to the material's existence and provides the immutable data for present and future speculation. Words, musical notes, and design sketches exist in space. We can see them. They are tangible. Their form and substance are frozen in the symbols on the manuscript. The brief and fleeting movement of dance exists in time, and during the vaudeville era it went unrecorded except in the muscle memory of the dancer or the kinetic memories of those blessed with them. The passage of time, the erosion of memory, and the absence of any permanent record of the dances themselves promote disagreement, dispute, and a record of wildly fluctuating interpretations of exactly what constituted the types of dancing indicated by the names of the steps and dances of the period. Nevertheless, some rough approximations can be made.

ECCENTRIC

In its original meaning, derived from the terminology of ballet, "eccentric dancing" issued from the talents and skills of the dancing comedian. Here the dancers put aside the ideal and universal standards of correct position and movement to pursue the humorous effects inherent in the ludicrous posture, grotesque behavior, or some peculiar physical mannerism of the dancers themselves. To say that the eccentric dancer eschews the correct and precise models of the *danse d'école* in no way demeans the skill and craft of the performer or the artfulness of the performance. The best eccentric dancers achieve theatrical effect by labor, forethought, and precise calculation. What distinguishes their dance commodity is the unique intent and direction of performances that grow out of specialized gifts and a highly individual dance personality. Think of Ray Bolger's awkwardly tall and lean torso tied to those splendid rubbery legs: The image defines the ideal outward shape and equipment for eccentric dancing, though Bolger's varied talents carried him beyond that narrow definition. To see what Bolger did with that equipment is to marvel at the dramatic, theatrical, or just pure entertainment goals that were achieved by such altogether unpromising means. Once established, however, eccentric specialties varied little from the original concept or the dance material derived from it. Early audiences expected that eccentric dancers would repeat their specialty regardless of context. Many did, and they did so to fame, acclaim, and financial success, like Fred Stone of the vaudeville team of Montgomery and Stone. In the words of a contemporary observer, Fred Stone's eccentric dance persona was that of "an acrobatic dancer . . . polished off with the art of the

This caricature of Ray Bolger accentuates his long, lean limbs, ideal equipment for eccentric dancing. (*Photo: Theater Collection, Free Library of Philadelphia.*)

mime and seasoned with the drolleries of the born clown." His specialty was the "gymnastic" dancing he developed from an early career in the circus, where he became an accomplished tumbler, an expert gymnast, and a daring rider. A contemporary reporter observed: "The first genius of Fred Stone is undoubtedly physical. Half the charm of his eccentric dances lies in the seeming ease and perfect rhythm with which he does the anatomically impossible." The nature of his routines carried over into his work in musicals as well. The most famous dance number that Montgomery and Stone ever devised was created for an operetta, *The Red Mill.* Fred Stone explained the routine and its genesis:

> I got the idea from working in a gymnasium. James J. Corbett was a member of the gym and used to work out there. He was a friend of mine, so I'd watch him. One day I told him that the footwork in boxing was just like dancing. So I taught him some steps and he taught me to box. The more I learned about boxing the clearer I could see what a knockout a boxing number would be in a show. So I invented one.
>
> In the dance Montgomery knocked me out, I went over backward, did a neck spin, slid across the stage on my head, then slid across again on my arm and finally came upright. At the end I was knocked backward again, went head over heels, like this, and came up in time to take a bow.

The reporter at the interview felt obliged to add that "as he talked, and during the last sentence, he did a cartwheel backward across the floor coming up to take an easy bow." Today, the eccentric dancer on Broadway would need to be a superstar of the first magnitude to have a theatrical property created specifically for the specialty or be lucky enough to stumble on a vehicle calling for that "once-in-a-lifetime-unlike-any-other" contribution. Should you now think that you understand the term "eccentric dancer," be advised that many dancers in early-twentieth-century American show business used the term in a completely different way, as when many of the tap dance greats of vaudeville, revue, and early musical comedy refer to Fred Astaire as an eccentric dancer. Since no definitive explanation accounts for the rather widespread practice, it must be assumed that any tap or acrobatic dancer who departed from the strict norms set by the closed society of its masters risked being labeled an eccentric dancer. Since *Webster's New World Dictionary* defines the word "eccentric" as "irregular; out of the ordinary . . . hence, deviating from the norm, as in conduct . . ." a strong case can be made for that theory.

COMIC

Only minor differences separated the eccentric dancer from the comic dancer. The eccentric dancer exploited personal characteristics of body and movement; the comic dancer relied more on character and situation as well as inherent physical tools. Invariably, comic dancers made their reputation by capitalizing on the noticeably heightened, highly theatrical properties of comic stereotypes: James Barton as a society drunk leaning against a lamppost, Hal LeRoy frisking about as a callow college freshman, Buster West's randy sailor, and Buddy Ebsen's country hick. The idea, the story, the character, and the situation made the act, even though some of the properties of the eccentric dancer figured into the execution of the material. Low comedy thrived on the vaudeville stage. Its audiences responded ardently to knockabout behavior that fell conspicuously below the norm. Perceptive dancers learned from the comics and devised comic dance acts with similar characters, situations, and structure. However, contemporary reviews imply an important distinction between the eccentric dancer and the comic dancer. All agree that both were funny, only the eccentric was funny for what he *was* while the comic was funny for what he *did*. Reviews of the famous eccentric dancer Jack Donahue usually begin with references to "the long, dangling legs of Mr. Donahue," or "Jack Donahue of the funny feet," or "Mr. Donahue's legs [which] are eerie and superhuman." The man was tall, about six feet, with angular proportions and limber arms and legs. He recognized his capital. Yet, when reviews tried to describe why the comic dancer James Barton was funny, they refer less to physical characteristics than to "his mimicry," "his steps," "his falls," "his slouches," and the character created on stage, who was a "bland chap in a nondescript suit that flaps about his limbs" who fell about the stage in drunken euphoria.

ACROBATIC

Acrobatic dancing, particularly the type called legomania, reached an unprecedented level of popularity and public acclaim during the era of the vaudeville specialty acts. Unlike the eccentric dancers, whose physical peculiarities promoted comic effects, or the comic dancers, who exploited character and situation for similar reasons, the acrobatic dancers relied on muscular strength or flexibility to execute the stunts, tricks, and feats of daring that kept contemporary audiences wishing for and getting more. For most, the inventory of tricks never changed: cartwheels, handstands, splits, backbends, front-overs, nip-ups, and somersaults. At worst, acrobatic dancing descended into the most vulgar displays of contortion; at best, it used the phenomenal flexibility built into its display to enrich and extend the boundaries of what dancers could achieve physically in all types of dance. How many Balanchine pas de deux explore the acrobatic capabilities of the dancers who perform them within the strict and demanding conventions of neoclassical ballet? In commercial show business though, the type of acrobatic dancing that endured longest was the phenomenon that came to be called legomania. Here, anatomy made the dancer. While the tricks could be taught, proper execution depended on flexibility of the joints of the leg. Essentially, legomania blended tricks of contortion based on how far apart you could spread your legs and what could be done with them in that position. Evelyn Law became a star merely for advancing across the stage on one leg as she shook her finger in mock accusation at the other, lifted high above her head in a six-o'clock position. Charlotte Greenwood's big trick was repeated hitch kicks to the side that appeared to allow the knees to graze, if not reach, the ear. That was all there was to it: high kicks to the front, back, and side, held in place or returned to the original position. Still, the popularity of its disciplines made legomania a staple

When the type of acrobatic dancing called "legomania" became popular during the era of specialty acts, Evelyn Law became a star by advancing across the stage on one leg as she shook her finger at the other. (*Photo: Theater Collection, Free Library of Philadelphia.*)

attraction in vaudeville, revue, musical comedy, and film. Another act that utilized acrobatic skills was man-woman teams that specialized in difficult and exciting lifts. These adagio dancers performed to the slow movements of classical or semiclassical music. Scantily clad, they built an act around beautifully sustained poses, precarious balances, and breathtaking lifts and twists. Modern variations of the adagio act persist in the Las Vegas–type nightclub revue.

Less visible on the modern entertainment scene are the ballroom dancers who employed many of the lifts and tricks of the adagio team but only within the context of a romanticized and highly theatrical interpretation of popular social dances like the waltz, fox-trot, one-step, two-step, and tango. The best of the elegantly clad ballroom acts not only reflected the social dance trends of the day but set them as well. Perhaps because they *were* a couple, the premier ballroom dancers of the

When social dancing became the rage on the musical stage, no act was more graceful, influential, and popular than the ballroom dance team of Vernon and Irene Castle. (*Photo: Print and Picture Collection, Free Library of Philadelphia.*)

era, Vernon and Irene Castle, danced as a couple. Dancing face-to-face in a position contemporary moralists thought to be vulgar, the Castles invented a new style of social dancing; it was intimate, natural, improvisational, and cleverly designed to be danced by people everywhere. Even if the Castles had not been the lovely, graceful, and ingratiating performers they obviously were, public accessibility to their manner of social dancing would have secured them a considerable success. But the Castles themselves were more than equal to their astounding innovations in social dancing. He was tall, slim, and a proficient dancer—the very model of a man ideally suited to leading the woman, as was normal social dance practice in that period. She was slender, graceful, and an equally proficient dancer—the most fashionable woman of her time and ideally suited to following her partner. Together the Castles changed how many Americans looked, dressed, and danced. Vernon and Irene

Castle had no rivals in their time, although other ballroom acts did sustain respectable careers, particularly if their act included the big trick of the "whirlwind." The term applied to the spectacular finish to a ballroom one-step or waltz that ended predictably in the applause-provoking whirlwind turns that climaxed many a Fred Astaire–Ginger Rogers film dance sequence. In addition to the ballroom acts, the vaudeville era spawned tandem acts performed by dancers of the same sex who dressed in similar costumes and makeup and executed the same movements precisely. In *Follies,* Michael Bennett choreographed a dramatically sound and theatrically effective tandem dance for different generations of performers in the number "Who's That Woman?" Critics and audiences blessed with kinetic appreciation recognized the practice by its latest name—the mirror dance.

Another cluster of show-dance acts popular during the vaudeville era were known by the adjectives that described the routine. The "rival" act developed out of the idea of a challenge dance. Virtuosic dancers from a male team like Mackin and Wilson or Welsh and Rice would alternate solo turns in an increasingly difficult or spectacular sequence of steps. The maneuver allowed each dancer the opportunity to surpass the efforts of the other before ending the routine by dancing off together. A rival act could be a "flash" act as well, but only if in the middle of the routine the dancers would launch without warning into a furious array of spectacular floor and air steps like the flip, spin, knee drop, or split. By contrast, a "class" act embodied all the grace, refinement, and elegance that an impeccably attired team could achieve dancing to slow music in either the ballroom or the soft-shoe style.

TAP

Of the modes of dance available to dancers during the vaudeville era, the most popular was the step dancing that came to be known as tap dance. Why? Black song and dance entertainers rose to prominence and popularity during the vaudeville era. Teams like Johnson and Dean, Williams and Walker, Buck and Bubbles, as well as solo performers like Bill "Bojangles" Robinson, set the tone and standard for the new, vigorous, and vernacular reinterpretation of the steps and dances that were the black dancers' heritage. On the vaudeville stage, black performers could show the artistic side of real personalities and not merely reflect the darky stereotype that prevailed during minstrelsy and thereafter. That black American tap dance evolved into a unique and long-lived show business commodity was due to an emerging black cultural identity that found a common, expressive language in the street tradition of step dances and to an increased acceptance of that dancing in popular American entertainment. The minstrel show disappeared, and minstrel specialty acts in vaudeville declined, but the dance tradition did not go away. Instead, waves of talented dancers learned in the long-established customs of the past embellished the old routines with the latest innovations from the back room or the street to form an exciting new hybrid of black dance parentage. The range of dance characteristics mirrored the range of dance personalities involved. Some tapped with the whole torso, some remained upright and rigid. Others deployed the hips and pelvis in sensual celebration, and a few even took to the air. Bill "Bojangles" Robinson brought step dancing up on its toes, and still others favored the hard, flat-footed style that took the sounds right down to the floor. To this day on the modern American musical stage, in new creations and revivals alike, the feet of Broadway dancers tap out the sounds that sing across the footlights as accompaniments to the music and as a complete and expressive aural message. But during the era of vaudeville specialty acts, no person delivered a more articulate or welcome tap message than the "King of the Tap Dancers," Bill "Bojangles" Robinson.

In many ways, Bojangles's career embodied all the elements peculiar to the majority of tap dance careers during the vaudeville era. Self-taught, lacking formal education, a natural talent with a famous specialty, the "stair dance," Bill Robinson tap-danced across the entire map of American show business for more than sixty years to unanimous critical acclaim and for salaries that climbed to approximately $6,600 per week for a 1937 appearance in motion pictures. In his day, the road to a dancing career in show business began in the street, literally. Robinson spent his childhood as a street boy who danced for pennies on street corners and in saloons. He never took a dancing lesson in his life. What he did with his feet was inherent, and he didn't know how he did it. The only consistent and predictable feature of his routine was the improvisational nature of the performance. He avoided formula, never froze a routine into a precise combination of steps, and took pride in never performing a routine the same way twice. He believed that tap dancing should be a natural and effortless expression of the rhythm inherent in music. A contemporary interviewer reported that he, "is dancing even when he is standing still, since the rhythms are still in his head, waiting to come out of his feet as a melody comes from the hands of a composer at the piano." The feet were his important concern, and he shod them for performance in what he called split-clogs. These dancing shoes looked like ordinary shoes, with a half sole of wood 3/8-inch thick and a wooden heel slightly taller than those worn on the streets of his day. A leather sole would be attached to the wooden sole from the toe to the back of the ball of the foot to permit maximum flexibility. The heavy, noisy, flat-footed tap style didn't appeal to him; delicacy became his forte. A *Chicago Daily News* review dated October 12, 1931, conveys the musical nature and delicate tone of his act:

> He begins with a flutter like drums, the sharp popping of firecrackers heard in the distance. Then his dance grows quieter and the audience leans forward to follow the tempo as though it were a thread of music. He skips a beat, two beats, three beats; they count and at "four" he picks up the rhythm inevitably.
>
> They give small gasps of satisfaction and strain again in utter silence to hear his pattering soles. He breaks time into bits but never drops that curious harmony and pattern of sound that winds through his dance like a theme. Now and then it is the steady beat of a race horse's feet, then a reverberation like a quail's wings. Sometimes it sounds like rain. But always each foot-note is precise, distinct, sure. Bill Robinson is as different from the shuffling levee hands as day from night.
>
> Four assistants bring out two sets of short stairways which, when put face to face, lead to a platform. Up and down these steps he keeps the rhythm going, never hurrying, never loafing, seemingly divorced from gravitation. He stops the light, drifting motion of his body and stands still; the clicking theme continues—done inperceptibly with his heels.

Robinson never departed from the fine, graceful, and easy style that was his trademark. While the flash acts around him accelerated the use of full-stage acrobatics or eccentric gymnastics, Robinson continued delicately to lay down taps with toe and heel like, as one writer put it, "the stroking of a fine pianist." Although he conducted classes at the Albertina Rasch studio, taught dancing with Ted Shawn to dancing teachers from every state, and granted private lessons to stars like Ruby Keeler and Eleanor Powell, Bill Robinson always came back to vaudeville. Despite successful engagements in musical comedy, revue, and film, Bojangles liked vaudeville best. He was first, last, and always a vaudevillian.

TOE

Although ballet had been popular with the "elite" American audience since the pre–Civil War tour of Fanny Elssler, its mode of expression proved too remote to most in the show business audience of the vaudeville era. Some ballet specialties did succeed, usually in the form of spectacular but vulgar allegorical ballets or divertissements with scenic embellishment and elaborate musical accompaniment or as acrobatic dance or legomania specialties performed in a manner that was then termed "toe dancing." Unlike the flood of tap dancers who learned on the street, danced their own way, and borrowed steps from each other, the toe-dance specialties studied dance from an early age, conformed at least initially to the rules of ballet discipline, and forged careers on dance material or skills peculiar to them. One such career belonged to the acrobatic toe dancer Bessie Clayton, whose big trick was a back-toe kick to the head while supported on the other foot. In 1915, when she toured the Orpheum Circuit with a lavishly costumed act, her big finish was a rendition of "ballin' the jack" on pointe.

But for many, vaudeville's premier dancers were Adelaide Dickey and John Hughes, who, as Adelaide and Hughes, toured the Orpheum Circuit with a series of "art" dances with names like "Birth of the Dance," "Classics of an Age," "Divertissements (in three parts)," and "The Garden of the World." E. F. Albee, head of the Keith Circuit that controlled the Palace Theatre, called Adelaide and Hughes "a model act," which he thought of as "one that constantly improves upon its material and continually introduces novel dances and effects." He neglected to add that the team played the longest engagement on record for vaudeville headliners at the Palace Theatre. "La Petite Adelaide," as the dainty dancer billed herself before teaming with John J. Hughes in about 1911, considered herself a ballet dancer of the European school, admirably trained and with an excellent technique. Although she and her husband-partner danced together in a variety of styles and modes, Adelaide turned to toe work for solos. Critical acclaim supported her incisive self-assessment that ballet accentuated her peerless grace and technique. Adelaide believed deeply in the value of ballet dancing and spoke out regularly on the subject, usually to advance her theory of ballet dancing as the only lasting kind of stage dance. She commented to the *Detroit Free Press* in September 1913:

The ballet is the outgrowth of centuries of evolutionary dancing. It is the highest point of dancing, just as opera is the highest point of musical composition and interpretation. The ballet dancer who takes her work seriously has to give it as constant study as a prima donna. There are fixed limitations to her art, but there is the compensation of a certain surety in working within these limitations. She goes by rote, but if she goes one inch wrong she knows it, and can correct it. She is, of course, in the classical school, but she knows that her school is the outgrowth of centuries of progress, and she knows too that there will be ballet dancers two hundred years from now as popular and as famous as are the great ballet dancers of today, as were the great ballet dancers of continental Europe two hundred years earlier.

The interpretive dancing then in vogue she dismissed as "novelties pure and simple," a "phase in modern theatricalism" that will last as long "as the popularity of the dancers." She believed that folk and ethnic dances needed to be given by people to whom they really mean more than attractive movement, exotic costumes, and show business novelty. In the same article, Adelaide said:

> The folk dances are just as much an expression of a national feeling as are the folk songs and tales, and they require the national sympathy for their presentation, just as it is required for the writing of a national hymn.

Apparently, Adelaide thought a great deal about dance in general and not just about show dance in particular. Twenty years before George Balanchine's arrival in the United States, Adelaide offered her assessment of the future of American dance and its dancers:

> I think that dancing is in the ascendant. While we of this country are not creative in art we take the forms and methods given us by the Old World and give them a new life and intensity. It is our zest and enthusiasm, our almost juvenile delight in what is new and daring that makes jaded and tired Europe care so much for us all of a sudden.

While Adelaide's theories brought her considerable publicity, only her act could sustain a successful career. Although she built her reputation in vaudeville as an "artistic dancer," there can be no doubt that she catered to popular taste. Popularity guaranteed success in vaudeville and Adelaide and Hughes knew it. A 1917 critic wrote that "years ago these dancers attained their goal and were acknowledged to be America's

The novel dances and theatrical effects introduced by the team of Adelaide and Hughes led vaudeville impresario E. F. Albee to call them "a model act." (*Photo: Theater Collection, Free Library of Philadelphia.*)

representative artists. Ever since that time, however, they have handled the frail craft, 'Success,' so skillfully that they have held it fast at the headwaters. The creative and technical ability of this clever couple is as great as their skill and grace." While knowledge and reason may have sustained Adelaide's provocative theories about ballet and American dance, cleverness sustained the phenomenal career that was Adelaide and Hughes. Adelaide herself watched other acts from the wings and checked out the competition. She disavowed all professional self-interest associated with the practice and claimed childish delight in watching a vaudeville show. Said she,

I take genuine pleasure in seeing the performances of the other actors. Sometimes, too, I gain inspiration for my own work; it is a great education in learning what audiences like.

What did vaudeville audiences want and get from Adelaide and Hughes? A September 4, 1917, *New York Telegraph* review by Sam McKee of their act at B. F. Keith's Palace Theatre:

These splendid dancers excel in telling stories through the medium of their speedy, easy grace, and the public wishes to see them exclusively during the brief time allotted on the program.

Always progressive, this season they have an entirely new series of dance interpretations, devised by their own thought and with special music by Leo Edwards. First, they are a dashing Broadwayite and a saucy miss of the Gay White Way. They fox-trot and waltz before, at the suggestion of Adelaide, whose petiteness is no way diminished by long ago dropping the adjective, they journey to toyland.

Following their whimsical toy impersonations, they flee from the storm in costumes similar to the familiar painting. Yet they do not flee as Paviowa and Mordkin did or as any one else has done previously. Adelaide and Hughes flee in rag-time.

Adelaide is winsomely pathetic as "The Last Rose of Summer," and Mr. Hughes is nobly impressive as a stalking red man, and their Japanese dance makes a dainty climax.

Adelaide and Hughes patronized their audience as did the majority of successful vaudeville acts; nevertheless, their success and the publicity it generated focused attention on "artistic dance" as an alternative to acrobatics, contortion, eccentric dance, comic dance, legomania, and tap. A perceptive critic writing in the December 9, 1914, *Columbus Dispatch* offered this estimate of their contribution: "[Their] entire offering is one no lover of dancing can afford to overlook." Although the dance directors of revue and early musical comedy would make more considerable and expressive use of toe dancing than did vaudeville, ballet movement as a popular mode of show dancing remained undersubscribed until George Balanchine and Agnes de Mille initiated the vogue for it with *On Your Toes* and *Oklahoma!*

OTHER INFLUENCES

Ethnic dance specialties of the more approximate than authentic variety inundated all forms of show business during the vaudeville era. Those dancers committed to the genre responded to the historical fact that theirs was an era of intense and widespread European immigration into the United States. Public performance responds to public demand, and the demand of many new Americans was for entertainment redolent of their homelands. If the singers and the comedians could exploit the audience of the American melting pot, then why not the dancers? So the parade began. Irish, Italian, Scottish dances, Indian dances, Dutch dances, Russian dances, and so on, and on, and on. At the time, the ethnic dance strain added little to the show-dance tradition. Later, authentic reconstructions of ethnic dances would flow so vigorously into the mainstream of American show dance that they redirected the course of dance mode, preference, and style.

Generous publicity promoted by the managements of the powerful vaudeville monopolies turned many talented dancers into celebrities whose every word and move were monitored by the press. As a result, teachers of dance, their students, and the general public found information available to them on the ideas, methods, background, and training of admired performers. Star dancers dissatisfied with the public's low level of kinetic understanding and appreciation used their celebrity to educate that public in the rudiments of their art. Interviews and feature articles began to focus not on what the dancer does but on what the dancer communicates.

One such dancer was Ray Bolger, the premier comic-eccentric dancer of his time and a pivotal figure in the transition of American show dance from virtuoso routines to expressive art. In his dances Bolger, tall and thin, with a phenomenally flexible body, assumed the character of an awkward, ungainly, and undistinguished man, seemingly uncoordinated but likeable. (The character of the Scarecrow in *The Wizard of Oz* is a codification of his style.) Commanding top dollar and admired by George Balanchine, no dancer of the time had better reason to indulge in the cult of personality and the success it assured. Instead, testimony culled from interviews granted throughout his career confirms a long-standing commitment to dance as serious business and expressive art. Bolger believed that "being a comic dancer is a serious matter," so he put ego, physique, and technique to the service of getting across whatever material he was given. The dance critic John Martin acknowledged the importance of the dancer when he pointed out that Bolger embodied in a comic mode the guiding principle of modern dance: All movement grows out of inner conviction. In Bolger's case, the inner conviction was so accurately attuned as to allow the performer freedom to improvise at will or under duress. As Ray Bolger told the *Saturday Evening Post* of July 30, 1949:

> I'm basically an actor playing the part of a little guy trying to dance. I mean, I'm a little guy expressing myself, only I happen to be dancing.
>   I don't know what I do, exactly. I never write down any of my routines . . . I completely forgot a routine I did last year. I just go out there and ad-lib. My wife calls me Ad-Lib Bolger.

Specialty dancers always pursued spontaneity and improvisation, but Bolger was different in that he opened himself up to ever-different ways of expressing character and situation in context. Earlier specialty dancers valued spontaneity and improvisation because they traded on tricks, eccentricity, or pure virtuosity. Their aims for dance were no greater than the best possible acceptance of dance itself.

An era that prized novelty, spontaneity, and individuality in dance performance allowed many dancers to maintain successful careers without the benefit of formal training. In lieu of the ballet, jazz, modern, tap, and ethnic classes widely available today, the young male specialty dancers learned their craft on the street, backstage, or on the job. Contemporary critics spoke of James Barton as "the greatest grotesque dancer in history," the "acknowledged expert on 'souse' comedy," the entertainer who "moved with every portion of his anatomy, made his quivering flesh and gyrating limbs sing songs, suggest poems in motion and do goodness knows what." Here is Barton on the subject of his background:

> I never had to learn how to dance, that was born in me. . . . Before I knew the alphabet I was out on the stages of variety theaters between shows practicing "breaks." My father and mother were both fine dancers and I would watch other performers on the bills and try to imitate them. By the age of nine I actually knew as much about tap steps as I do today. The only difference is the number of years during which time I have practiced constantly.

Similarly, the eccentric dancer Jack Donahue began his career as a kid in Charlestown, Massachusetts, where he danced on street corners for pennies thrown by passers-by. On the other hand, the women who sought dance careers during the vaudeville era entered the profession with a suitable, if not impressive, dance background. The contemporary standard: Dance class for girls, yes; dance class for boys, no.

The dance specialties of the vaudeville era thrived in an eclectic entertainment milieu and responded to naive, undiscriminating audiences. Professional dancers lived for applause, and applauded dancers lived very well. A lifetime career could be sustained by a repertory of twenty steps, with an additional six or eight more intricate ones for encores. Dance entertainers had arrived, even if their art had not.

4

The
Dance
Directors

Between the specialty dancers who originated routines from the raw material of their own talent and the pioneer choreographers who viewed movement as expression for communication stand the dance directors of early musical comedy and revue. Their professional ascendancy coincided with that of the vaudeville dance specialists, although philosophy, aesthetics, and function separate the two into clearly different categories. The specialty act provided the main attraction; dance directors devised the most suitable and imaginative context for that act. Generally, producers hired the dance director to audition and train the chorus dancers, devise novel and exciting dance backgrounds to enhance the stars, and dream up the elaborate costumes, sets, and special effects that distinguished the dance routine from others like it. No art here, just commerce, and no dance director could be of better service to a producer than one who could consistently and unerringly give the audience what it wanted. The recipe for commercial success included the following ingredients: (1) popular stars, (2) beautiful girls, (3) comedy, (4) memorable songs, and (5) dance numbers that stopped the show. The producers bought the ingredients; dance directors arranged them into an attractive package. The system bound everyone involved to the endless quest for novelty. Where modern choreography strives for expressive, particularized movement, dance direction strove for clever new ways to present the old routines. Figuratively speaking, dance directors brought to each new project a well-worn little black book of routine steps. Creative speculation amounted to little more than which routine to put here and which routine to put there. Why not? After all, the production did feature new dancers, new costumes, new sets, new songs, and new

41

lighting. Although some in the audience may have noticed the standard recurrence of steps and combinations, few seemed to care. Those who did were a group of aspiring choreographers who shared a more ambitious and artistic notion of what show dancing could do and what special role it might play in the overall American entertainment scene. None was more outspoken than Jack Cole. *Dance Magazine*, April 1949, printed this Jack Cole response to the title "dance director":

> This title is used to designate the man who arranges the musical numbers for a show where the music is loud, rhythmic and brassy; the girls are pretty, and meet all *Esquire* conformation standards; the shoes have either spikes for heels or metal plates on the toes, the costumes are flattering and a joy to the chorus, and the feathers are stuck casually in the customary places. The dancing associated with this type of show usually bounces with rhythm and bursts with vitality, is not too carefully filled in with detail or too tiresomely rehearsed. A calculated air of spontaneity is aimed for that sometimes leaves the audience with a suspicion that all this may be happening for the first time.

Probity demands that that uncomplimentary assessment of dance directors be accompanied by a statement of the incontestable fact that these talented, imaginative, and often innovative dance makers worked in American show business at a time when the performers as well as the public viewed dancing as a bright and welcome garnish to more substantial theatrical fare. Much needed to change in the philosophy and composition of the shows themselves before anyone could risk the inevitable creative and practical hazards of inventing new and vital movement during the four-, five-, or six-week rehearsal period. If the producers themselves assembled shows from unrelated fragments of story, score, comedy material, and star turns, why shouldn't dance directors mix and match their proven, if unrelated, movement fragments into diversions both described as and designated by the word "routine"? Any dance director with a grasp of dance fundamentals could build a dance routine in the old tradition: He picked out eight to ten steps from his repertory, assembled them in ascending order of difficulty, and saved the most flashy, unexpected, or unusual item for the end—applause had to be provoked. Once dance directors discovered the format that worked best for them, they applied it indiscriminately. That most successful and influential early dance director, Ned Wayburn, arranged dance routines in sequences of ten steps: Step One was the entrance, a traveling step to

During the 1920s, the dance directors of Broadway and Hollywood relied on precision dance routines made up of simple steps executed within a variety of geometric patterns, as in this scene from *The Broadway Melody*. (*Photo: The Museum of Modern Art Film Still Archives.*)

bring the dancers onto the stage; Steps Two through Nine were a combination of eight steps and kicks executed in a variety of angles; and Step Ten was the exit step, designed to climax the routine for audience applause. If the routine stopped the show? Good. If the audience demanded an encore? Better still. What the modern director-choreographer seeks to advance, the dance director sought to interrupt. Oscar Hammerstein II expressed little longing for the old days when he pointed out that "the more the dancing made the audience forget, for the moment, what the story was about, the more successful it was!"

The majority of dance directors subscribed to the notion that precision dancing constituted the right and proper action within the chorus line formation. Whether performed on taps or toe, the precision dance routines demanded an undeviating execution of steps and the willing subordination of the individual personality to the homogeneous look of the chorus line. Since audiences responded best to machinelike uniformity in performance, the dance directors relied on simple steps within a kaleidoscopic array of geometric patterns. The practice prospered. So captivated was early-twentieth-century American show business with the

vogue for chorus girls put through quasi-military drills that many a
Broadway musical featured an "imported" precision troupe in addition
to its regular dance chorus. Dancing schools responded to the demand
for nameless, faceless dancers by producing decades of nameless, faceless
dancers. For the dance director, building a good number had less to do
with the dancers on whom it was built than on some novel approach,
trick, or technical package for the routine that would distinguish its
discipline and uniformity from the discipline and uniformity of the
others. Occasionally, a contemporary critic complained:

> In recent years the intensive application of hard work has given a machine-
> like precision to the dancing in musical comedies, or at least that is the way
> the tradition runs. Young men and women are so often put through the
> hopper of the present-day dancing schools without particular attention to
> personalities that one chorus performs almost exactly like every other. Each
> kick seems somehow to be stretched to a uniform height. The tricks of
> dancing are so universally known that audiences are said to pay little or no
> attention to them. "Good numbers" just about expresses the gist of critical
> comment.

Precision dancing prevailed nonetheless.

The tradition of precision dance in American show business began
in about 1910 with a fad for the unison marches and folk dances that
first appeared in the amateur shows of a wealthy English manufacturer
named John Tiller. Tiller's amateur productions led to professional
theatrical opportunities on the London stage and the opportunity to
open the school for dance that would supply precision troupes of eight
or sixteen dancers for London musical productions. In America Oscar
Hammerstein I imported a troupe of John Tiller Girls for productions at the Olympia Theatre, as did producers like Charles Frohman,
George White, Charles Dillingham, and Florenz Ziegfeld. When the
producer of a musical show signed a contract with Tiller for a precision
troupe, Tiller himself would assemble the dancers for the complete unit
and appoint a unit manager charged with responsibilities that ranged
from all financial arrangements for the group to mediation of personal
disagreements among the members. The troupe arrived in America
complete with two or three fully orchestrated routines ready to be added
to those to be devised for the new production. The Tiller troupes were
trained in a variety of dance techniques, although the later troupes
abandoned toe dancing for precision steps and kicks performed in
American-style tap dance. The "Tiller system" produced all the dancers

in the troupe, for Tiller believed that his prolonged and intensive method of training raised English female chorus dancers far above those in any other country. Whether products of John Tiller's London dance school or the branch operated in Manchester, England, by his son Lawrence, Tiller Girls began training at an early age and continued instruction until show dancing became second nature to them—a process that lasted at least ten years. When John Tiller arrived in New York in 1912 to accompany his girls during engagements in New York, Chicago, and a short season of vaudeville in the middle west, he revealed the details of their education and training to the press:

> The training begins when the child is nine years old. . . . Of course all of the pupils are not that young, but I prefer to start them at that age. The English law will not permit children appearing in public until they are ten years of age. The first training is in the hands of Mrs. Tiller and her assistants, and it includes considerably more than dancing. The children are taught the usual school studies by certified governesses. They are impressed with the importance of personal cleanliness, of regular hours, and of good morals. Their hands and feet receive particular attention, because of course a dancer must have strong feet. In most cases I try to separate the children from their old home life, for in most cases their homes may not be of the best.
>
> The first period of training lasts about a month, and then a weeding out process takes place. Of course we have to discard a great many applicants at the very first trial, but at the end of the month we are in a position to know what sort of material we have. I should say that about 60 percent of the pupils stand the test at the end of the first month. The training then continues, on an average, for about a year. Some of the pupils show unusual aptitude, and they are advanced more rapidly than the others.
>
> Usually the first engagement a child has is in pantomime at Christmas time. When they go into the theatre their training does not stop. In the mornings they must be ready for school at nine o'clock, and their instruction is continued by the governess. She accompanies them to the theatre in the afternoon, where there are two performances a day, and the schooling goes on between the acts. The children must have at least six hours of lessons a day. They are taught a little drawing—and some of them show considerable talent. One of the Palace girls who is with me in this country now is really a very good artist. They have their music, too, and the rudiments of vocal instruction.

Often, training continued during appearances on the road and during every new production. The uniformity in type, training, and performance so admired by critics and audiences alike was due to the fact that the same set of girls remained together for years and profited as a unit from personal familiarity and continuous practice. Tiller revealed in a contemporary interview that

> I have girls in some of my companies who have been with me for over twenty-one years. There is one in America now who began her training when she was eight years old and she is now twenty-nine. She doesn't look much more than twenty. And you know a girl does not keep her good looks and her youth if she does not live carefully.

Eventually, American dance directors entered the field and assembled their own troupes for the growing market. The repertory of the Gertrude Hoffman girls featured acrobatic numbers and synchronized fencing drills along with standard fare like high-kicking routines. (Hoffman was a vaudeville dancer who did popular versions of the modern dance presentations of Loie Fuller and Isadora Duncan.) A novel specialty was web dances in unison, in which the troupe performed acrobatic figures on giant rope webs. The Gertrude Hoffman girls represented a brave, new, athletic manifestation of the American chorus girl. One contemporary newspaper account held that their new look combined the best features of the Tiller method with the method of Isadora Duncan of "California, Paris and Moscow." The hybrid generated a chorus style that embraced precision (Tiller) and freedom (Duncan). In Europe, however, a Gertrude Hoffman troupe scandalized Paris audiences with the latter, particularly the "abandon" and "recklessness" of this new approach to the show dance chorus. On Broadway, rival dance directors guided their dancers farther still from the European model. For three decades they presided over the evolution of American show dancing from precision drills to expressive movement and over the evolution of dance creators from dance directors to choreographers. Their names were Ned Wayburn, Albertina Rasch, Seymour Felix, Busby Berkeley, Bobby Connolly, and Robert Alton.

To assess the climate of show dancing in the first three decades of the twentieth century, no more effective and telling barometer exists than the career of Ned Wayburn—the most prolific, outspoken, and influential dance director of his day. His career spanned forty-one years, more than six hundred staged productions in New York and London, and an incalculable number of vaudeville acts. The most prominent producers vied for his services; he staged and directed musicals for five years with

Ned Wayburn directed Donald Kerr and Elise Bonwitt in this scene from the 1920 musical comedy *Poor Little Ritz Girl*. (*Photo: Courtesy of Rodgers and Hammerstein.*)

Klaw and Erlanger, five years with the Shuberts, and seven years with Florenz Ziegfeld. His best-known stagings included *The Passing Show of 1912*, *The Passing Show of 1913*, *The Ziegfeld Follies* from 1916 to 1919 (and again in 1922 and 1923), and the Lew Fields musical comedy *The Poor Little Ritz Girl* (music by Richard Rodgers and Sigmund Romberg, lyrics by Lorenz Hart and Alex Gerber). In 1905 he founded a school of dance "more closely allied with the actual professional world of dancing than any other institution" that offered the "all-round training demanded by every important manager, producer and stage director today." The Ned Wayburn school promised "Health, Beauty, Fame, Popularity, Independence." His courses were practical, too, incorporating as they did all "the essentials of modern stage dancing, but without the grinding training methods and without long years of study on a single technique." The Ned Wayburn Institutes of Dancing in New York and Chicago "trained" the male and female dance chorus engaged for Wayburn shows. It also allowed its famous founder to coach and therefore take credit for such stars as Fred and Adele Astaire, Evelyn Law, and Gilda Gray. Presumably with the consent of its founder and director, the school brochure listed the names of internationally famous stars "whom Mr. Wayburn has directed and helped up the ladder of fame." Predictably, the list reads like the *Who's Who* of American show business during the first three decades of the twentieth century. Although "their careers have been moulded on the basic qualities of their personalities," Ned Wayburn allegedly guided and inspired Eddie Cantor, Al Jolson, W. C. Fields, Marilyn Miller, Marion Davies, Ann Pennington, Will Rogers, Vivienne Segal, and no fewer than 122 other stars.

Since Wayburn appeared on the entertainment scene early in this century, he embraced the aesthetics of precision dance. Observers noted that his dances incorporated these characteristics and standards: "intricate steps and rapid motion," "perfect unison," "exact execution," "smiling dancers," and poses and groupings that appeared to be "second nature" to the performers. Ned Wayburn the pedagogue divided American show dancing into five categories: musical comedy dancing, tap and step dancing, acrobatic dancing, exhibition dancing (ballroom), and modern Americanized ballet. Professionally, Wayburn preferred the musical-comedy dancing style he called "fancy dancing," an idiom composed of "pretty attitudes, poses, pirouettes and the several different types of kicking steps that are now so popular. . . ." For him, fancy dancing represented a cross between the pretensions of ballet and the rhythmic vigor of tap and step that could: (1) enhance all height groups of the chorus, (2) adapt to any stage area, and (3) provide aspiring dancers with a repertory of the "neat routines" preferred by his associates as well as his competitors. For efficient communication in class instruction or rehearsal, Wayburn divided the stage into performance areas and movement into direction or angles. The ground plan of the "modern theatre stage" at the top of the following page, prepared for his book *The Art of Stage Dancing*, illustrates his breakdown of the total space of a stage into twenty-four separate areas. To explain movement within those performance areas, Wayburn devised a theory of eight directions as indicated by the figure at the bottom of the following page from the same source.

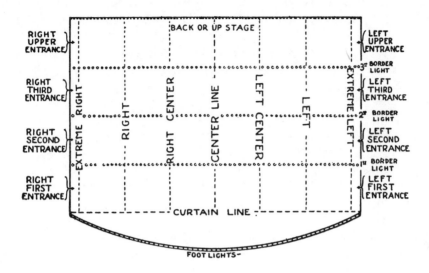

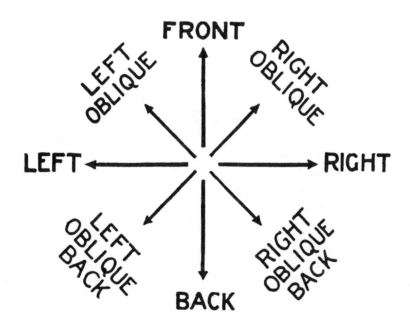

For dancers who could count, recognize stage areas, and understand angles of movement, Wayburn charted musical comedy routines, like this dance in 4/4 tempo to the tune of "Way Down Upon the Swanee River":

WAYBURN'S MUSICAL COMEDY ROUTINE: 4/4 TEMPO
TUNE: "WAY DOWN UPON THE SWANEE RIVER"

The dancer enters from stage left.

Step right foot to right oblique on count of "one." Step left foot behind to right oblique back on count of "two"; step right foot around behind the left on count of "and"; step left foot to right oblique on count of "three"; repeat same for "four," "five," "and," "six." Step right foot to right oblique, count of "seven"; drag left foot in air behind to right oblique and slap left heel with right hand on count of "eight."

Step left foot to left on count of "one"; drag right foot in air behind to left oblique and slap right heel with left hand on count of "two"; step right foot to right on count of "three" and drag left foot across in front in air on count of "four"; step left foot to left facing left, count of "five"; right foot front small step on count "and"; step left foot back facing back, count of "six"; right foot to left, small step on "and." Left foot to right facing right, count of "seven"; right foot to back, small step on "and." Left foot to front facing front, count of "eight." Now repeat entire movement.

These two movements should take the dancer to the center of the stage; done in eight measures of 4/4 time.

Step right foot to right oblique count of "one"; hop on it in same place with left foot in air behind to left oblique back, count "two"; step down to left oblique back with left foot on count of "three"; hop on left foot, extend right foot in air right oblique on count "four"; step right foot back behind left foot on count "five"; step left foot to left oblique back, count "six"; step right foot across to left oblique, count "seven"; hop on right foot, extend left foot in air right oblique back, count of "eight." Now reverse this entire movement to other side. These two steps are done in four measures 4/4 tempo in the center of the stage.

Step right foot to right, count "one"; step left foot behind to right oblique back, count "and"; step right foot down in same place, count "two." Reverse to left for count of "three," "and," "four"; then step right foot to right, count "five"; step foot in front to right, turning and facing up stage, count "six"; step right foot around stage front to right, turning front again, count "seven"; drag left foot across in front of right to right, count of "eight." Reverse this entire step to other side. These two steps are done in four measures of 4/4 tempo in center of the stage. This finishes the first half of the chorus, or 16 measures.

Facing left oblique, drag right foot from left oblique to right oblique back, count of "and"; hop on left foot in same place, count of "one"; drag right foot from right oblique back to left oblique, count "and"; hop on left foot same place, count of "two"; drag right foot from left oblique to right oblique back, count "and"; hop left foot same place, count of "three"; displace left foot with right foot from right oblique back, left foot extending to left oblique, all on count of "four." Hop on right foot same place, count "and"; step left foot to left oblique, count "five"; step right foot across in front to left oblique, count "six"; hop on right foot same place, count of "and"; step left foot to left oblique, count of "seven"; hop on left foot same place, and turn, kick foot to right oblique, count "eight."

Going up stage right oblique back facing right oblique, step right foot back to right oblique back, count "one"; step left foot to right foot, count of "and"; step right foot to right oblique back, count "two"; step left foot to right foot, count of "and"; step right foot to back, facing back, count "three"; hop on right foot turning right to face front on count of "four." Step left foot to left oblique on "five"; step right foot to left foot on "and"; step left foot to left oblique on "six"; step right foot to left foot on "and"; step left foot to left oblique on "seven"; hop on left foot and kick right foot to right oblique on "eight." Reverse all of these steps. These are done in eight measures of 4/4 tempo in the center of the stage.

Step left foot to left oblique, count "one"; step right foot behind to left, bend left knee, count "two"; hop on right foot and kick left to left oblique, count "three"; swing left foot back to right oblique back on "four"; bring right foot around behind left on count "and"; step left foot to front, count "five"; step right foot back to left on "six"; bring left foot around behind right on count "and"; step right foot to front on count of "seven"; step left foot to left oblique on count "eight."

Step right foot to right on count "one"; swing left foot up stage and step to back on "and"; right foot straight in place, facing up stage, count "two"; step left foot to stage right on count "three"; facing right swing right foot to right, count "and"; step left foot straight in place, count "four"; now facing front, having made complete left back turn. Now step right foot to right oblique back, count "five"; step left foot to right oblique back behind right foot, count "and"; straight with right foot in place, count "six"; step left to left oblique back, count "seven"; step right foot to left oblique back behind left foot, count "and"; straight with left foot in place, count "eight." Reverse these steps.

These steps are done in eight measures of 4/4 tempo, in the center of the stage.

This completes the first chorus, or 32 measures.

In addition to setting down routines, the Wayburn method codified the kicks, turns, and poses to be inserted into them. For the front kick, the dancer kept the supporting leg straight as the other rose straight up without bending at the knee. The term "hitch-kick" applied to kicks designed to reach fourteen inches over the head. The back kick demanded that the working leg be bent at the knee as it rose to kick the back of the head. Ideal execution called for the simultaneous action of head and shoulders back in a deep backbend with a vigorous backward thrust of the kicking leg. When performed sequentially, the front-and-back-kick combination became a "pendulum kick." To perform a "fan kick" the dancer traced a complete circle with the extended leg. The majority of Wayburn routines favored front kicks to the front, right oblique, or left oblique. For contrast, he used turns, either simple, single movement turns, or the four one-quarter turns suitable to unison dancing in large formations. The inventory of poses ranged from the conventionally formal and erect to the more dramatic bent-torso lunges. The composition of the musical stagings employed many of the geometric figures used today: the straight line, the rectangle, the circle, the arc, and Wayburn's trademark, the V of the triangle. To move the dancers into and out of these figures, Wayburn directed movement into "paths" that resembled the shape of a W, a serpentine coil, and a bisected circle. When, in an early edition of the Ziegfeld Follies, the designer Joseph Urban devised a setting with uncommonly steep risers, Wayburn averted possible catastrophe for the showgirls by devising a unique walk that allowed the elaborately costumed Ziegfeld Girls to negotiate the staircase safely and in comfort. Performed at an oblique angle, the movement featured a highly stylized walk in which the forward thrust of the shoulder balanced the forward thrust of the opposite hip. So, in response to a technical problem, Ned Wayburn gave the world the famous "Ziegfeld walk," which appeared in many of the subsequent Follies.

Imagine yourself perusing some promotional material from a long-since-defunct show business enterprise. The format is that old standby of the advertising business: Before and After. Before is a graceless, overweight, and countrified young woman wearing a carelessly braided pigtail down her neck, the most awful party dress imaginable, and an appropriately unbecoming demeanor, After is the same girl, but this time she appears slim, poised, sophisticated, elegantly gowned, groomed, and posed in a much earlier era's interpretation of a "come-and-get-me" attitude. Anyone curious enough to express interest in the agent of such miracles gets rewarded with an answer: the *Ned Wayburn Institute of Dancing*. Although Wayburn used a male chorus in many of his shows, their function was decidedly subservient—background for female stars or soloists. Primarily, New Wayburn was in the "girl business," onstage and in the classroom. Speaking of training young women for the stage, Wayburn said:

> It is necessary that every feminine form be as near perfect as possible in order to attract the attention of the eye of the audience as well as the ear. In our school we make it a business to produce beauty. Neither sentiment nor art enters the question—it is purely a commercial proposition with us. Audiences will not come to the box office with their money to see ugly, misshapen girls on the stage. Therefore it is up to me to make them right. This means hard work for pupil and teacher.

He divided his girls according to height and function and gave each category a name. For "show girls" he chose tall, willowy girls of exceptional facial beauty. Although he expected them to know how to dance, he preferred in them an ability to sing and to wear the fabulous costumes designed for them only. The shortest girls were known to everyone in the business as "ponies." "Ponies" danced, often and well. Sandwiched between the extremes were categories of dancers he called "chickens" and "peaches." Whatever the category, Wayburn insisted that his dancers possess an inherent sense of rhythm abetted by professional training—preferably his. For him, rhythm meant "coincidence of movement and music," and he boasted often of his ability to recognize that talent in his dancers:

> I can tell by the way a person walks across the floor when an orchestra or any musical instrument is rendering a sprightly bit of dance music, whether or not the walker has the dancing sense that is so necessary to perfection in the art.

Once a candidate was accepted, the average time for study and career preparation lasted about six months. Although Wayburn's concept of training appears shallow and undemanding by today's standards, he was one of the first to recognize the importance of overall physical culture to dancers bent on a career in show business. He advised all dancers to rest, sleep, relax, and exercise. Odd exhortations in his time; prudent advice for today.

When a group of trend-setting dance directors succeeded Ned Wayburn in prominence during the 1920s, they improved the standards for dancers and musical staging within the inherited and still unquestioned "bring-down-the-house-and-stop-the-show" philosophy of dance routines. The job of dance director hadn't changed as much as the names and the faces in the rapidly changing show-business landscape. The theater programs that advertised "dances and ensembles by Bobby Connolly" merely called attention to the man who supervised "the leg and ankle work" and devised the trick dance routines for such shows as *The New Moon, Funny Face,* and, particularly, *Good News.* That David Bennett "staged" the ensembles for *Rose Marie* and *Sunny,* among others, meant that he "told the chorus girls what to do with their hands and feet" and decided what they all would do in groups of from eight to twenty-eight dancers. The quest for novelty persisted. Busby Berkeley admitted, "I always strove to do the unusual—something they didn't expect." Bobby Connolly, originator of the "Varsity Drag" in *Good News,* attributed the popularity of the dance to its ability to catch the public's fancy. He theorized:

> This is an age of enthusiasm, speed and strenuous undertakings, and the popular dances merely reflect, or rather express the predominating moods of life as it is lived today. . . . The people of today are ever on the lookout for something *new,* and that gives dance creators their opportunity.

Although expectations regarding dancers and dancing improved, vestiges of silly criteria remained. David Bennett revealed these rigid requirements for his dancers during an audition for a Paramount Studios motion picture: "To get into my chorus . . . a girl must be close to five feet four inches in height and weight from 105 to 115 pounds. In selecting girls from those who meet these height and weight requirements, I look first at their teeth. Good teeth are the initial beauty essential of the chorus girl." In another interview, he elaborated on his standards for dancers: "I have always chosen girls with the idea, first, of getting healthy ones. Posture has much to do with my selection. If a girl doesn't sit well, I know she has let herself become slouchy. She probably has been too lazy to brace herself properly at the waist, where vital organs are." Busby Berkeley was in the beauty business and attributed his success in the beauty market to an ability to please the public with his product. A contemporary newspaper account, "Feminine Beauty is Dance Director Busby Berkeley's Business," bares his impersonal approach to the selection of dancers for his chorus:

> Berkeley, therefore, has put beauty on a business basis. He regards the horde of gorgeous creatures who apply to him for jobs, and the comparative few who get jobs, the way a nut-and-bolt manufacturer regards his products.
>
> When Berkeley looks at a girl, he looks at her face and her figure. He looks at her arms and hands, watches the way she handles them. If they're beautiful but handled clumsily, she's "out." If they're all right, he looks at her legs. And they have to be good!

Fortunately, Bobby Connolly's requirements for the chorine included some mention of dancing. He preferred physically attractive, slender, five-foot-three to five-foot-nine body types who could "do a little buck dancing, toe dancing, acrobatic dancing, high kicks, splits and character dancing so that they might be able to participate in every ensemble in the show." Surprisingly, he did not believe that these dancers needed training from an early age. Although he admitted the benefits of extensive early training for the soloist, specialist, or star, he contended as well that a chorus girl with a fairly natural aptitude could be taught to dance ensemble work in the four weeks that happened to be a musical show's rehearsal period under early Equity rules. Contemporary press releases revealed the secret of his success: "He treats the girls like sisters and he knows every Broadway show girl by her first, middle, or nick name. He even knows the real names of some."

A rival dance director named Sammy Lee disagreed with Connolly's complacency toward dancer training. For him improvements in the musical shows themselves demanded more strenuous, intricate, and acrobatic routines that only skillfully trained dancers could master. Undoubtedly, increased competition among the many new girls who sought stage careers during the liberated 1920s helped raise lax and stringent standards alike. Sammy Lee reported that "for the chorus of former years a stage manager could select one out of three applicants: but I tried out more than a hundred girls before selecting the dancing octette in *The Gingham Girl*."

Though none of the trendsetters influenced the course American show dancing would take, each made some lasting contribution to its treasury. David Bennett originated the domino routine—a surefire contrivance made use of by many of Bennett's contemporaries and successors—for ending a dance number, which consisted of lining the girls up in a row, allowing the first to fall over, causing each member of the line to fall over sequentially. Bobby Connolly made tap dancing popular by favoring its use in chorus routines. LeRoy Prinz broke the unison effect of the chorus line by selecting different steps for different dancers in the line, an accomplishment as much a reflection of sophisticated spatial manipulation as a clever division of labor among dancers of unequal ability. Prinz called this technique the "conglomeration effect" and described it as "a matter of every dancer going to town and doing something different usually for the last sixteen or thirty-two bars of music." Busby Berkeley broke up the line, too, but by character devices, not spatial manipulation. Contemporary observers credit him with "tampering" with the unity and precision of the chorus line by introducing "the little girl at the end of the line," who, as the perennial underdog who had to work harder and kick higher to fit in, was a surefire avenue to laughter, sympathy, and applause. We can see vestiges of this gimmick in most modern ice shows, which include a little girl (or boy) at the end of the line who must catch up with the others to complete the formation and so win the affection of the audience. More sophisticated than this were Berkeley's experiments with multiple rhythms. When so inclined, he would set tap routines for dancers counting in 3/4 or 5/4 time to music played in 4/4 time, thereby creating the novel aural sensation of a dance filled with shifting accents and interesting syncopations.

Historically concurrent with but creatively ahead of the trendsetter dance directors were the innovators Seymour Felix, Albertina Rasch, and later, Robert Alton. Of the three, Seymour Felix, who choreographed the Rodgers and Hart shows *Peggy-Ann* (1926) and *Simple Simon* (1930), was the earliest to express publicly a more creatively ambitious, theatrically integral, and dramatically motivated vision of show dance than had ever been encountered on the commercial dance scene. Not that he eschewed completely the pretty girls and the dances designed for public consumption. Rather, he dared to believe that after a level of achievement consistent with contemporary standards, more should be demanded in his profession so that more could be achieved. Like his best contemporaries, Felix sought dancers with youth, beauty, and a strong dance foundation. He preferred very young girls by today's chorus standards, girls who ranged from sixteen to eighteen years of age who were products of ballet or other dancing schools. His reason? After the age of twenty, dancing girls lose their "pep" and the "youthful effervescence" that makes a chorus so attractive. And was *he* selective! At the first chorus call for *Peggy-Ann,* four hundred girls responded. He chose four. Said he: "It seems almost impossible to find capable girls, girls who have looks, who can dance and who are willing to go through a strenuous routine." To his credit, Seymour Felix recognized as a dead end the cult of novelty and tricks that dominated the show dancing of his time. When necessary, he could pull out the old stops with the best of them: high kicks, backbends, splits, cartwheels, military drills, the chorus line strut that stopped the show, and the double time Charleston that left the onlooker breathless. Uncharacteristically, Seymour Felix was not blind to their limitations. He assessed his professional milieu and the practices it encouraged with uncommon accuracy. "It was all very lovely, all very interesting," he admitted, "until the bag full of tricks was emptied." Prophetically, Felix sensed that the future of stage dance rested in an improved station within the total creative process. He reasoned that:

> the best high kicker can kick no higher than the length of her legs; the daintiest, most graceful of young women can only dance a Charleston or a Black Bottom when she is supposed to dance a Charleston or a Black Bottom. In many instances, the chorus interlude became a colorful but negative interruption to the action or comedy of the musical comedy book.

This was not Agnes de Mille or George Balanchine talking about the prospects for theater dance in the late 1930s or early 1940s. This was Seymour Felix discussing his work for *Peggy-Ann* in 1926. What could possibly have accounted for such insight, daring, and vision? Was it the stimulus of working with Richard Rodgers and Lorenz Hart or Herb and Lew Fields? In any case, Seymour Felix set himself thinking about dance that "aided development" and kept in "the spirit of the show" a full decade before the earliest recognized commercial work of the pioneer choreographers. During his work on *Whoopee,* Felix declared to the press, "No longer are routines a matter of speed and noise. . . . The cycle of acrobatics, 'hot' dancing, and stomping is over. . . . Scrambled legs have become a bore. The important thing today is the so-called 'book number.'" Having convinced Florenz Ziegfeld, the producer of *Whoopee* that "it is the story that counts," Felix set about to devise "atmospheric" numbers, dances that unfold gradually and consist of development and climax as if they were dramatic units themselves instead of "a mere pounding of feet and kicking to music." Colorful dances could be, and spectacle they could embrace, but harmonize with the story they must—and did. Then as now, the secret to successful integration of show dances lay in the discovery of valid motives for the movement. Often, Felix discovered valid reasons for the dance in dramatic atmosphere. For *Simple Simon,* Felix created a dance to elicit the social environment of Coney Island as it would appear then to a typical sightseer. In *Peggy-Ann* he utilized stage properties to create the stage pictures that supplemented the story of the show. A contemporary newspaper account attests to his innovative, book-oriented staging of the "Hello" number from *Peggy-Ann*:

The problems of Seymour Felix in the presentation of the dance numbers in the current intimate show, "Peggy-Ann," were not lightened by the character of the entertainment. The first scene of "Peggy-Ann" is played as a rural comedy. The setting represents the living and dining room of an up-State boarding house. Six characters who are introduced must be established in their various identities for the sake of the dream sequence which follows.

The room parallels a porch for two-thirds of its rear wall. Within its three walls and the mythical wall represented by the footlights, Clark Robinson designed a setting which lacks nothing in detail. It contains a piano, a settee, ten wicker chairs, an arm chair, a curio cabinet, a tabouret and a dining room table. Into this room Mr. Felix had to place twenty persons—two principals, six boys and twelve girls of the ensemble.

He also had to create an atmosphere, the atmosphere of holiday merrymaking, in contrast to the mood of Peggy-Ann, who is not allowed to go on a hayride by her mother and who stays home to dream the wild melange which forms the greater part of the musical play.

Dancing was nearly impossible. Formations were limited to a small space in the centre of the room and the line just back of the proscenium. The result of a week's rehearsal, however, introduced a new element into the number: the utilization of properties on stage for the creation of stage pictures. A special dining room table was obtained, under which eight of the ten chairs in the room fitted. A light wicker settee, easy to move, replaced the original overstuffed conception which Mr. Robinson had suggested.

Mr. Felix then proceeded to create stage pictures, which supplemented the story of the play. His girls enter and listen to the principals as they sing the refrain of the Richard Rodgers–Lorenz Hart song quite as if they were overhearing a conversation. They greet the boys with a cheery "Hello!" they dance a bit, and finally they begin a series of flirtations, the girls with Jack Thompson, the boys with Margaret Breen.

The ten chairs and settee are moved about, screened by a line of dancers, with the result that the furniture actually dances. Mr. Felix's victory over chairs and tables is almost an epic one, for the "Hello" number is warmly appreciated by "Peggy-Ann's" audiences.

Once he recognized the dependence of the dance ensemble on book, music, and lyrics, Felix sought to ensure a more unified effect onstage by coordinating his efforts with that of the show's creators. These pioneer attempts at dance integration elementary and ingenuous as they must have been represent a major step forward for commercial dancing. At last, dance was thought of as part of and not apart from the major collaborative elements of a show. The efforts of Seymour Felix on behalf of show dancing did not go unrewarded: In his time, he was reputed to be the highest paid dance director in the business.

Although what we know of her dances and dancers does not invite critical scrutiny by today's standards of concept or execution, Albertina Rasch's sensitivity to the total dance world of her time—a sensitivity that nourished uncommonly experimental show dancing—demands that she be included in the society of innovative dance directors. Hers was a commercially successful career built on a traditional ballet foundation, one that spanned three decades of American show business and included such major critical and commercial hits as *Rio Rita* (1927), *The Band Wagon* (1931), and *Lady in the Dark* (1941). A bright young pundit on the contemporary scene even spoke of Broadway "breaking out in a Rasch." Why the success? Why the adulation? Albertina Rasch came to America at age sixteen with nine years of training in the ballet school of

Albertina Rasch created the "White Heat" number for Fred and Adele Astaire in the 1931 hit revue, *The Band Wagon.* (*Photo: Theater Collection, Free Library of Philadelphia.*)

the Imperial Opera Company in Vienna. She danced in opera ballets in New York and Chicago, toured South America with Sarah Bernhardt, and trouped across the United States regularly with a graceful and endearing vaudeville act. When the time came for Albertina Rasch to teach and direct, she was prepared with a wealth of dance and theatrical experience all the more effective for one additional asset: a gift for organization. Unquestionably, Mme Rasch used the position of dance director to make the "fancy dancing" of ballet a salable commodity in popular American show business. Her girls and their dances reflected the contemporary affection for mechanical precision without always subscribing to the tyranny of movement in unison. When Rasch combined the characteristic features of ballet movement with the new, syncopated dance steps set to modern music, she originated a hybrid style unlike any previously encountered by American audiences. Instead of setting the traditional high kicks, splits, backbends, and acrobatic tricks to ragtime and jazz, Rasch prescribed synchronized jetés, snappy relevés, and breathless tours jetés. It was a simple recipe for so considerable a success: Just put the European ballet vocabulary to the service of the "semibarbaric" dances of America. Calling her type of dancing "American ballet," she trained troupes of dancers called the Albertina Rasch Girls. They were a sensation. Not only did Mme Rasch interpolate her girls into a dazzling succession of Broadway operettas, musical comedies, and revues, but she exported them as well to European cities like London, Paris, and Berlin as ambassadors of the new American style. Unlike Seymour Felix, Albertina Rasch made little attempt to integrate dancing into the creative process of putting on a show. True, she worked to make the dances fit, but as decorative interpolation, not from organic or artistic necessity.

The Albertina Rasch dancer aspired to requirements and standards that differed considerably from the contemporary mode. Although their teacher and mentor demanded youth, grace, and well-formed physiques, more was expected than physical perfection alone. Because she herself came from a European ballet academy, Mme Rasch believed facial beauty to be secondary to the ability to make audiences experience the beauty of the dances, and that dancers so gifted possessed a "gleam of radiance," a "power of expression," and the very "essence of beauty," which meant the power to stir the imagination. Paradoxically, Rasch the teacher encouraged individuality in her dancers. She valued technique but not without the personal expression needed to communicate the message of the dance to an audience. Consequently, dancers whose qualities of intellect or personality separated them from the others received her

Albertina Rasch trained troupes of dancers called the Albertina Rasch Girls for Hollywood films like *Rosalie* (1937). (*Photo: The Museum of Modern Art Film Still Archives.*)

attention and allegiance. "I can always dress them up," she said, "but when they have brains—ah—but half my battle is won." Not surprisingly, Rasch prescribed standards for professional behavior as well:

> There are other important qualities that I look for in my young dancers: courage, resourcefulness, good nature and fairness. These are requisites for success in any art, profession or business, but especially in a career as full of work, disappointments, pleasures, achievements and glories as the life of a dancer.

Like Ned Wayburn, Albertina Rasch believed in appropriate training for dancers in show business and devoted considerable effort to promoting herself as the foremost teacher of stage dancing in America. Unlike Wayburn however, Rasch realized that proper training demanded time, patience, discipline, and the ongoing support of the young dancer's family. She cautioned the dancers and their families to be patient while preparing for a career. While endless rehearsals might produce the mechanical perfection associated with the chorus girl, only time and study could produce a *dancer*. A full ten years before the arrival of George Balanchine, Albertina Rasch recognized the extraordinary potential of American dancers and spoke often of their superiority over their

European counterparts. In her view, not only had America taken the lead in ballet work, but had developed a unique style as well. Said she, "America is now among the leaders in ballet and other dance work. . . . Indeed, I do not hesitate to assert that America is the leader." Albertina Rasch admired the American body and the commitment of its dancers:

> And nowhere in the world are there as apt pupils as in the United States. The girls excel in every way women of foreign birth, and it won't be long, I feel confident, when foreigners will turn to us for instruction. We are developing a ballet of our own, using the technique of the masters, and are giving zest and life to our undertaking.

Albertina Rasch formulated these convictions for commercial dance. They do not differ substantially from the convictions that brought George Balanchine to the United States to found a school and build the company that would become the New York City Ballet.

The line of important and innovative dance directors ended with Robert Alton, whose prolific career extended well beyond the era of the pioneer choreographers. In fact, Robert Alton may well have been the most prolific dance director on the Broadway and Hollywood scene during the 1930s, 1940s, and 1950s, with such shows to his credit as *Anything Goes, Pal Joey,* and *Me and Juliet.* Unlike his contemporaries, Alton held tenaciously to the tap-dancing style of an earlier era at a time when show dancing began to discover a new movement vocabulary drawn from ballet, modern, and ethnic dance. Openly acknowledged working methods that incorporated no research, little planning, and discovery by chance made him an anachronism in a show dance milieu occupied by George Balanchine, Agnes de Mille, and Jack Cole. A contemporary newspaper clipping reported:

> Alton never plans his numbers ahead of time, believing it best to let them work themselves out during the preparatory period. First, he has the music played several times to get the rhythm and tempo; then he memorizes the words, and with these fixed in his mind he tries to interpret in dance form just what the lyric means.

When a reporter from another newspaper asked how a dance director creates routines, Alton replied:

> It's the last thing I think about. First I study the book. Then I consult with the scenic designer and the costumer. We exchange ideas. With all this

Bert Lahr poses with the dancing girls of the 1939 production of *DuBarry Was a Lady,* dances by Robert Alton. (*Photo: Theater Collection, Free Library of Philadelphia.*)

firmly in my mind I call a rehearsal. I say "Do this." And it's a step. I don't know why. It's always been that way. And, brother, I hope it always stays that way.

My poor memory for dancing comes in handy because in that way, I rarely repeat myself.

Robert Alton made no adjustments in style or methodology for his work in Hollywood films. When in 1952 the Hollywood reporter Richard Dyer MacCann asked Robert Alton to explain his "way with a dance," the dance director replied:

I study the script, listen to the music, and then go away and dream about it for a while. When I have the ideas I need, I get together with the designers, begin rehearsals, and work out from there the final arrangements of both dances and music.

It's just as simple as that. The ideas come, and I put them to work.

Now, I never sit down and search for an idea. You can't force these things. I remember once Richard Rodgers and Larry Hart turned over to me, in desperation, a first act ending. I just let it go and tried to keep it out of my mind, as a "problem."

Robert Alton re-created this vaudeville song-and-dance act for the 20th Century-Fox production of Irving Berlin's *There's No Business Like Show Business.* (*Photo: The Museum of Modern Art Film Still Archives.*)

Then one day it hit me, just as I was stepping into a cab. I stood there, halfway in, for 30 seconds, while the whole scene unfolded, in my thought. Then I got in and told the driver where I was going.

The characteristic Alton mode of show dancing used tap dance as a stylistic base onto which elements of ballroom, ballet, folk, or ethnic dance could be grafted. So entrenched did this image of show dancing become that the scholar Cecil Smith identified Alton as "the truest and best representative in our time of the historic qualities of American popular theatre dancing." Like so many of the musicals in which his dances appeared, Alton offered audiences bright, sexy, and happy dancing unencumbered by serious purpose or symbolic meaning. He sensed what the audience wanted and gave it what it liked. "I am a commercial man," he announced proudly. "I have exactly six minutes in which to raise the customer out of his seat. If I cannot do it, I am no good." In order to "do it," Alton often spent fourteen hours a day whipping up sixteen or seventeen dance numbers in four weeks for a New York show. His standards for hoofers were high, and he proudly admitted to being "very snooty" when it came to hiring dancers. To maintain professional standards, Alton auditioned "everybody in town," weeded out from long-running shows dancers who had put on weight or lost motivation, and maintained a constant lookout for new talent for future shows. As a maker of dances, Alton was gifted with an uncanny sense for matching steps to music, a technical characteristic that demanded consistently high levels of talent and energy from his dancers. All the whispers at an Alton audition echoed the word that had already gone around for years: "You've got to be good, because he's really tough." An anecdote from Alton's Hollywood days confirms that suspicion. Columbia Pictures brought Robert Alton to Hollywood to stage the dances for *You Were Never Lovelier,* starring Fred Astaire and Rita Hayworth. As Hollywood reporter Lucie Neville reported,

> Some 300 hoofers, notified by Central Casting, answered his chorus call, but a lot of them didn't stay—just sneaked out when they saw the steps required.
>
> Conclusive proof of his standards is that after the first day's rehearsal, the chorus went on strike, saying in sulky astonishment, "This is specialty stuff! We aren't going to work for chorus wages. No movie director ever asked us to do these steps." Screen Actors' Guild officials, after watching a routine, agreed and ordered their salaries raised to that of specialty dancers.

In no production were the Robert Alton routines more appropriate or well received than in *Pal Joey* (1940), the show that Richard Rodgers

Robert Alton gave audiences bright and happy dancing, as in this routine for principals and chorus from Rodgers and Hammerstein's *Me and Juliet,* 1953. (*Photo: Courtesy of Rodgers and Hammerstein.*)

regarded as "the most satisfying and mature work" to emerge from the Rodgers and Hart collaboration. That year the dance critic John Martin wrote in the *New York Times*:

> Robert Alton, who created the dances for the show, has given . . . dancers some corking things to do. The routines themselves are nicely characterized and worked into the scheme of the whole. Musical comedy devotees have not forgotten the stunning first-act finale which he staged for that other George Abbott show, "Too Many Girls," or how he made it part of the general action. Here his assignment has been altogether different and far more subtle, but he has taken advantage of the opportunity just as fully to make his numbers an integral part of the proceedings. His dream number in which Joey visualizes the night club of his ideals, the wonderfully common "Flower Garden of My Heart," the witty hunting dance, and the ingenious and comic "Do It the Hard Way," are delightfully smart and flavorsome. Indeed, the whole production is so unified that the dance routines are virtually inseparable from the dramatic action.

To be sure, Alton's work benefited from director George Abbott's strong guiding hand in "molding music and lyrics, setting and costumes, dancing and acting, into a hilarious instrument for translating into stage terms all the implications that John O'Hara put into the original sketches of Joey. . . ." Whoever was responsible, the dance material of *Pal Joey* represents one of the earliest successful examples of concept as form. The dancing in this show depicted their environment and projected character without any diminution of the brassy entertainment values then prized in musical shows.

To his credit, Alton believed in total body movement over dancing that emphasized footwork alone, and his choreography for Gene Kelly in *Pal Joey* reflects that conviction. The tap dancing for sound effects alone that so concerned the "true" tap dancers held little eye value for Alton. The ballet-tap style of the show did not escape the attention of John Martin. Of the Gene Kelly–Robert Alton contribution he wrote:

> In his dancing he quite evidently makes use of the principles of ballet technique, chiefly in its relation to the oppositions and balances of the various parts of the body. He has a natural lightness and excellent elevation, and could without doubt become a good ballet dancer if he put his mind to it. He has not let the ballet hybridize his tap-dancing, however, but uses it apparently because tap-dancing does not of itself supply any natural means for the use of the upper body.

This problem is one of the most important ones that the tap-dancer has to solve.

As a professional, Alton believed in frequent chorus rehearsals during the run of a show to keep his dancers from becoming too mechanical in execution or straying from the initial spirit of the routine. Reviewing his professional theories and opinions, one discovers a few convictions that set him apart from the past. It bothered Alton that the show dance contribution received insufficient coverage and criticism in the press. In a 1940 *New York Times* interview conducted during a break in rehearsals for the musical revue *Hellzapoppin,* Alton discussed the problem:

> The dancing in a musical often takes up more than half the time of the entire performance, it represents days of hard work and gruelling rehearsals for the boys and girls and, nowadays, is an important asset to any show. But somehow recognition is slow in coming and I do believe straight-forward criticism and recognition of this work would help the dancers as well as the director. There is nothing quite so good as criticism to improve the work of an artist.

Later in his career, Alton recognized the limitations of staging the dances in a book musical only. He had announced as early as *Anything Goes* a determination to "pick up pointers in straight direction with the goal of ultimately directing the book and the dances of a musical comedy."

In no way did the innovations and contributions of all these dance directors prove typical of their milieu. If what was best in their work seems painfully limited, what was typical of the others only deserves the enlightened disregard of subsequent generations. In all fairness, the dance directors labored under handicaps that explain the limitations of their product and their methods. One: Early audiences had little knowledge of dance technique and training, much less any expectation of dance as an expressive medium. Two: The questionable nature of dance instruction and the widespread conviction that beauty and talent alone qualified a dancer for the chorus forced many of the dance directors to work with limited dance resources. In any case, the professional impact of dance directors diminished in direct proportion to the rise of collaborative choreographers like Balanchine and de Mille. The growing presence of ballet and modern dance on the American entertainment scene presented the new dance makers with bold and exciting options as to the type of dance employed and its function within the overall design of a show.

When opportunity knocked, three pioneer artists answered.

VISIONARIES
AND
MODERN MASTERS

Pioneer Choreographers

GEORGE BALANCHINE

Prior to the opening of Rodgers and Hart's *On Your Toes* in 1936, the man responsible for the dances requested that his program credit read "Choreographed by . . ." rather than the customary "Dances by. . . ." The producer agreed. The prospect of arousing public curiosity over an unfamiliar word opened up intriguing new avenues for valuable publicity. So did George Balanchine fire the first salvo in a revolution that would change forever the nature, scope, and function of American show dancing. Balanchine began his career with impeccable training at the Russian Imperial Ballet School in St. Petersburg, followed by early choreographic opportunities in his native country and then in the West with Serge Diaghilev's Ballets Russes. Thus, by training and by temperament, he was inclined to regard dance as an expressive medium and a serious art. As in the work he was doing with the fledgling Ballet Society, for stage Balanchine created dances, not routines. He insisted that his work for the commercial theater be integral to the show's intent, not merely its decorative accessory. Earlier dance directors like Bobby Connolly, Seymour Felix, and Albertina Rasch had sought to connect their dances with some element of the show itself, usually the lyrics, but as Oscar Hammerstein II pointed out, these primitive attempts at dance integration helped the show in "an oblique way" only. Instead, Balanchine's choreography for *On Your Toes* contributed vital information to the unfolding of the plot in repeatedly entertaining demonstrations of how viable dance expression could be as a method for advancing story by means other than song or scene. When the show was revived in 1982, Carol Lawson reported in the *New York Times* that:

71

On Your Toes was a turning point in the history of musical comedy, for Mr. Balanchine's dances were more than mere interludes. Instead they served as essential aspects of the plot, and were thoroughly integrated parts of the production.

Unfortunately, the original *New York Times* review dated April 13, 1936, focused exclusively on the dancing of the performers, particularly the extraordinary contribution made by Ray Bolger. Aside from reporting that the show included "a dry burlesque of the Scheherazade ballet, and . . . a melodramatic ballet entitled "Slaughter on Tenth Avenue," the reviewer devoted no critical space to the maker of the dances or the dances themselves. The only other mention of Balanchine appeared as follows: "Scenery by Jo Mielziner, costumes by Irene Sharaff, choreography by George Balanchine, staging by Worthington Miner—all O.K., high class and sublime." On the other hand, the same day's *New York Herald Tribune* review gave dance far more critical attention:

> The episode which caused an uproar Saturday night at the Imperial was called "Slaughter on Tenth Avenue." In it Mr. Bolger danced frenetically because he had been told that if he ceased his activities he would be shot by villains sitting in an upper box. While these sinister figures, lit up by green

George Balanchine choreographed the melodramatic ballet entitled "Slaughter on Tenth Avenue" for *On Your Toes* in 1936. (*Photo: Courtesy of Rodgers and Hammerstein.*)

spotlights, threatened him with destruction, Mr. Bolger danced desperately, beginning with jazz's simple single taps, thence proceeding to triple hoof-beats and flights of soaring. It was a triumph of rhythm and alacrity over the static romance of Times Square comic opera, and the cool first-nighters found much warmth in it.

Again, Ray Bolger's contributions dominated the review. Contemporary critics made no effort to distinguish the dancer from the dance. More disturbing, however, was the fact that George Balanchine was not named or discussed in the body of the review, only in the opening credits that listed the names of the collaborators. "Choreography by George Balanchine" was all the mention he received.

The plot of *On Your Toes* deals with backstage life in the ballet world; that was new and "foreign" material on Broadway in the 1930s. Consequently, the audience proved as unprepared as the critics for the dancing—its importance to the show itself and its impact on the shows that followed. When the tongue-in-cheek send-up of the ballet *Scheherazade,* or *A Thousand and One Nights,* entitled "La Princess Zenobia" was performed in the original production, the audience simply didn't know how to react. Many missed the point altogether, and the few who didn't were too polite to laugh outright. Yet, when the revival played a very successful London run in 1984, the *Christian Science Monitor* reported that the "audience wiped tears from its eyes from laughing so much."

Although his predecessors had employed toe dancing successfully in vaudeville, musical comedy, and revue, Balanchine opened the door for ballet on the commercial stage at a time when the mindless American musical was about to give way to the serious musical plays of Rodgers and Hammerstein, Lerner and Loewe, and their contemporaries. The classic American musicals that erupted on the Broadway scene during what musical director and composer Lehman Engel called the "great period" of the 1940s and 1950s embodied unequivocally romantic ideals in content, spirit, and form. If their songs could raise the audience to a higher artistic level than speech alone—so bestowing on the theatrical moment the emotional power to soar above the concerns of the real world—then no mode of dance could be better suited to this type of theater than ballet. The heart of the traditional classical ballet experience is linked to the sensations of grace and pervasive ethereality achieved by dancers trained to execute athletic feats of enormous difficulty with a demeanor at once quiet, relaxed, and serene. Could any mode of dance be more appropriate for Laurie in *Oklahoma!* (1943) and her figurative and literal need to fly out of her dreams and into Curly's arms? Tap dance: too rhythmic and percussive. Modern dance: too uncompromising and cerebral. So successful and pervasive did ballet become on Broadway after Balanchine and de Mille that the phenomena just about erased jazz-tap from commercial musicals and put many of its virtuoso performers out of big-time business. Temporarily, American show dancing had turned its back on what the adherents of tap called the "real American dance."

More important to the show dance tradition than the specific choreography Balanchine contributed to such shows as *On Your Toes, I Married an Angel, Babes in Arms, The Boys from Syracuse, Song of Norway,* and *Where's Charley?* was the model he became for the complete choreographer—the flawlessly trained master of movement who thinks exclusively in terms of dance. Expressive movement has assets unavailable in the assembled steps of a routine. Where routines divert, dance invites. Choreography treats the invited audience to kinetic commentary along with the kinetic excitement of the dance. Although George Balanchine chose to devote his choreographic energies to neoclassical ballet, his work in commercial dance demonstrated the bold and exciting options open to choreographers of show dancing, as well as contributing images and rhythms to his ballets. From that moment its prospects escalated gradually and then frantically toward later manifestations in

Jimmy Savo falls for Wynn Murray in a Balanchine ballet from Rodgers and Hart's *The Boys from Syracuse,* 1938. (*Photo: Courtesy of Rodgers and Hammerstein.*)

Agnes de Mille began the trend for dream ballets in Broadway musicals with "Laurie Makes Up Her Mind" from *Oklahoma!, 1943. (Photo: Courtesy of Rodgers and Hammerstein.)*

the choreographer-as-director and the choreographer-as-creator of a musical show.

AGNES DE MILLE

Agnes de Mille joined the revolution in 1943 with choreography for *Oklahoma!* that functioned onstage in so substantial and valid a way as to secure for the choreographer the status of coequal to playwright, composer, and lyricist in the making of a musical show. It also began a trend that would litter the show dance landscape of the 1940s with integrated ballets. In the year following *Oklahoma!,* twelve of the twenty-one musicals produced on Broadway contained a ballet or some reasonable facsimile thereof. Within eight years of the advent of George Balanchine and *On Your Toes,* ten of the dance makers for those shows listed themselves as choreographers while only two held onto the growingly obsolete title of dance director. Of the seventy-two musicals produced during the next three and a half years, forty-six included ballet, and twenty-one offered dream ballets, often with "staggering ineptitude." *The New Yorker* reported:

This trend may have reached its lowest level with the appearance, in September, 1945, of a dream ballet in the musical "The Girl from Nantucket." After enduring this, one critic remarked sorrowfully, "Around a

Jud Fry's Post Card Girls brought to life by de Mille's choreography for *Oklahoma!,*
1943. (*Photo: Courtesy of Rodgers and Hammerstein.*)

rather elderly young man . . . raged a furious ballet led by a trio of dancers
representing the sea, the whale, and Tom, a somewhat seedy fisherman. On
my card, the whale was leading on points right up to the knockout, but it
was quite a bout. There can be no question that Agnes de Mille has had a
great and on the whole virtuous influence on choreography, but her example
has led to a great deal of innocent suffering, too, this being the most acute
specimen up to now."

At her best, de Mille fashioned dance dramas for the commercial stage
that developed out of plot and advanced the action of the story. Her
dancers appeared as characters in the show and not merely impersonal
instruments for dance entertainment. De Mille assigned her dancers
dramatic features previously reserved for actors and singers only—among
them depth of character, motivation, and emotional content. If character
is the soul of drama, then casting dancers as characters opens up new
horizons for the dancers and the drama. The dancing Laurie and the
dancing Curly add to the total dramatic impact on the audience begun
by their acted and sung counterparts, just as the dramatically established

In "The Farmer and the Cowman," de Mille used gesture, position, and lifts to enlarge on *Oklahoma!*'s emotional and intellectual content. (*Photo: Courtesy of Rodgers and Hammerstein.*)

characters of Laurie and Curly give their dancers background and motivation for expressive movement. All the great ballet companies prior to Balanchine's own established the fusion of dance and drama in performance as a major artistic priority. *Oklahoma!* brought that fusion to the popular stage. Suddenly gesture, movement, steps, turns, and lifts acquired layers of suggested meaning that were as indicative of the show's emotional and intellectual content as what the composer's musical notes connoted aurally. That was an important moment for show dancing as well as theater. When imitation and parody hastened the demise of Agnes de Mille-era choreography, Walter Kerr offered this reappraisal in the *New York Herald Tribune*:

> What has been lost, for me, is emotion. At its best, current stage dancing has impact—a cold-blooded, calculating, haymaker thrust that is essentially concerned with keeping the "entire production" plunging onward. But nowhere to be seen—except in the somewhat imperfectly restaged movement of *Brigadoon*—is that sudden, almost imperceptible, moth-like flutter of life that starts with the barest movement of the actors' bodies, flickers for a moment on the verge of definition, and then is—before you have caught the miracle in the act—deeply involved in stating some of the more touching truths of everybody's life. It happened in *Oklahoma!*, it happened between James Mitchell and Gemze de Lappe in *Paint Your Wagon*, and it happens when the girls lightly sweep away from the walls in *Brigadoon*.

Agnes de Mille aimed to enlighten the audience with her choreography for *Brigadoon.* (*Photo: Theater Collection, Free Library of Philadelphia.*)

Such dancing talks to the audience across the footlights. It says things like "here we move the plot forward," or "here we establish the tone and atmosphere of the scene," or "here we explore some of the ideas built into this situation or setting." Dance directors worked for audience approval; choreographers work for audience enlightenment.

The new aspirations of show choreography brought with them additional responsibilities for its dancers. Dancers had always interpreted ideas and feelings on the commercial stage, but it was usually their ideas or feelings as stars, soloists, or chorus actively engaged in the joy of dancing. Agnes de Mille set her dancers the task of projecting characters, not themselves. The dancers may have drawn resources from the well of their own feelings as do actors in comparable situations, but a dancer's individuality projected through personal response to the music or setting would no longer do for the integrated musical. As a result, the new show dancing demanded that the choreographer provide the dancers with as much direction borne out of script analysis and character motivation as do stage directors rehearsing actors. Predictably, de Mille would assume the responsibility of director for Rodgers and Hammerstein's *Allegro* (1947), a project whose promises none of the collaborators adequately fulfilled.

To the growing repository of show-dancing accomplishments Agnes de Mille added a more expansive approach to stage space for the dancer.

Agnes de Mille's movement for *Carousel,*1945, illustrated the dramatic situation for audience enlightenment. (*Photo: Courtesy of Rodgers and Hammerstein.*)

The cast of Rodgers and Hammerstein's *Allegro,* 1947, moving to direction by Agnes de Mille. (*Photo: Courtesy of Rodgers and Hammerstein.*)

An expansive use of physical space characterizes this moment from the film of *Carousel*. (*Photo: Courtesy of Rodgers and Hammerstein.*)

In *Oklahoma!*, the idea of open spaces and the blue horizon should be realized in more than merely appropriate settings for the time and place of the play. Open space should function throughout the show as the guiding metaphor for the promise of the American dream and the limitless opportunities for the "brand new state" and the lovers destined to inhabit it. De Mille's conception of the dances for *Oklahoma!* reflects that conviction. Rodgers and Hammerstein, who combined robust music with lines like "plenty of room to swing a rope/plenty of heart and plenty of hope" in the title song, recognized de Mille's rendering of that vision in her appropriate and expansive use of physical space. Early in the dream ballet "Laurie Makes Up Her Mind," the dancing Curly sustains the dancing Laurie in a lift that seems to go on forever. Although subsequent dances alternated solos, trios, quartets, and larger groupings, the dancers never looked crowded, the stage never looked cluttered. Particularly notable was her effective choreographic use of the diagonal line to give an impression of depth and perspective. To the vigorous and robust dynamic quality of the dances, achieved by continuous movement, de Mille harnessed a ballet-oriented movement mode characterized by open body positions and generous extensions that evoked a feeling of endless space and air. The best theater art promotes immediate audience acceptance of the unreality before them, the so-called "suspension of disbelief." The artistry of de Mille's dances for *Oklahoma!* was such that its audiences forgot that what they saw was actually happening within the confines of a theater.

Intellect, research, and choreographic skills account for Agnes de Mille's achievements. Advance preparation involved script and score analysis complemented by intensive study of the styles, manners, mores, and dances of the period. The motive was to acquire a concrete grasp of background, authentic flavor, and local color. Unlike dance directors, choreographers aspired to an artistry based on *interpretation* through expressive movement that eschewed duplication or reproduction. Along with such avid intellectual curiosity, fed by research and preparation, came the technical understanding of a trained dancer and the proven skills of a successful choreographer of ballets such as *Rodeo, Fall River Legend,* and *Three Virgins and a Devil.*

By the time she arrived on the Broadway scene, de Mille had already developed a unique, eclectic style as well as an extraordinary talent for character definition and storytelling in dance. Just as songs in the integrated musical possess the complete and well-molded forms of puzzle pieces that can build the overall picture, so de Mille's dances were formed to stand on their own as complete works and still contribute to the greater demands of an entire production. De Mille believed strongly in dance integration and had to struggle throughout her career to secure its best interests. An anecdote associated with the preparation of *Bloomer Girl* illustrates the point. At one stage in the rehearsal process, the composer Harold Arlen informed de Mille that the show needed a ballet "to bridge a gap in the second act between the outbreak of the Civil War and its ending." As *The New Yorker* reported the story:

> Miss de Mille, whose husband was just then involved in the liberation of the Continent, thought she knew exactly what was indicated. She went home to her apartment, stayed there four days, and emerged with a complete ballet, one of the three she did for the show. It opened with some girls saying goodbye to their men, who were going off to war. Then the body of a dead soldier was brought onstage, and after a ballet sequence, the widow of the soldier was left standing alone beside the body. Miss de Mille was pleased with her effort ("a rushing, running thing, with a steady beat that sounded

like the wind," she has since called it), but when, after several rehearsals, she showed it to E. Y. Harburg, who staged the show and wrote the lyrics for it, he shook his head and told her it was too stark for a musical. "I'm not going to do an *Oklahoma!* barn dance about a war, if that's what you have in mind," Miss de Mille said sharply. Harburg said that, no, he didn't want that, either, and proceeded in a soothing voice to suggest some changes, the foremost being the elimination of the dead soldier. Harburg's proposal called for the ringing of victory bells and was, in Miss de Mille's words, "all very Fourth of July—war was over, nobody died, and peace was declared in ten minutes." She refused to accept it, and for a while it looked as if a stalemate might result, like the one involving Uncle Cecil and the bull. Finally, Miss de Mille, after composing four versions in four weeks, was persuaded that the soldier's body wasn't an essential part of a sombre scene, Harburg agreed that the Fourth of July touches should be toned down, and the compromise ballet struck several of the critics as the best part of *Bloomer Girl.*

Why did she battle? Why did she persist in her views? Said she:

> What every choreographer looks for is an opportunity to do what he wants without grave interference and curtailment. In our theatre, it's not possible, if you are just a choreographer. You run afoul of the director and the author and the composer, except in unusual circumstances—such as *Oklahoma!* where all of us seemed to breathe with the same pair of lungs.

At one time in the early 1960s, de Mille believed that the interference of other collaborators may have been financially as well as creatively motivated:

> The plain truth is the producers won't recognize us as a union, and behind them are the authors and the composers and the scenery people, and they don't want to divide up anything with anyone. They don't want to be crowded. They will not take us in as collaborators unless they are forced to.

For de Mille, the process of making dances began in private. By herself she might try to picture each character moving to music in some singular way, perhaps in costume or bathed in stage lighting. In this way she hoped to discover some appropriate choreographic image that might be released from the encounter. In response to dramatic situation, a character's posture, gesture, or movement could serve as a basis for, or as a beginning to, dance construction. To embody the kinetic images so derived, the choreographer chose dancers adept at projecting character as well as performing steps. Dancers under de Mille's supervision attest to her uncanny avility to sense a dramatic nature in their performance personalities, to draw out those expressive qualities, and then to integrate them into choreographic sequences through trial-and-error dancer collaboration. As a result, de Mille's dancers exhibit strikingly appropriate personalities onstage. Her method draws out the elements of characterization from the dancers themselves and does not impose some desirable artifice on the dancer or the dance. Dancers who achieved critical recognition because of this approach support the method. The satisfied include the *Who's Who* of stage dancers in the 1940s and 1950s, among them Bambi Linn, James Mitchell, Joan McCracken, and Gemze de Lappe. Unfortunately, choreography so derived rarely suits the understudies, the second cast, or the road company dancers as well as it does the original dancers. De Mille herself admitted that the original dances would not look the same in performances by subsequent dancers. In addition, some detractors have claimed that de Mille exploited the original dancers by using their freely given ideas, gestures, and movements—and by taking credit for them. To gain some perspective on that accusation, one must focus on the choreographer's artistic objective as well as her method. De Mille worked with dancers the way a director works with actors. Her dancers were expected to contribute; that is, they were expected to collaborate on characterization just as actors are expected by directors to bring something of themselves to the process of building a role. Should dancers playing characters be given their performance, or must dancers, like actors, discover their performance in rehearsal under the guidance of the director-choreographer? In addition to a facility for interpretation, de Mille made technical demands on her dancers so that the strenuous choreography would not be compromised in performance. Katya Sergava danced the role of Laurie in *Oklahoma!* for twenty-nine months, during which she endured fifteen different partners, many of them forced out of the show with incapacitating injuries.

Since Agnes de Mille entered the world of commercial dance as an adult artist, she recognized (1) the limitations of choreography generated by ideas other than one's own; (2) the severe restrictions of rehearsal time mandated by union contracts; (3) the space and movement compromises needed to accommodate the scenery, actors, and singers mandated by others; and (4) the inevitable hysteria associated with the hothouse atmosphere of an enterprise characterized by too many cooks working in a very hot kitchen. Personally, she realized and accepted both the subtle and overt manifestations of discrimination bound to affect a woman of her time working in a profession dominated by men. The wise, tart, and feisty Agnes de Mille responded to the challenge with the same resources she channeled into her choreography. Only achievement would guarantee parity, and it did.

JACK COLE

If George Balanchine was the consummate Russian-American ballet master moonlighting in show business until he could establish the company that became the New York City Ballet, and if Agnes de Mille—whose background was in modern dance—was the literate and accomplished mistress of characterization in dance appropriately disposed to the storytelling pretensions of the musical play, then who and what was Jack Cole? A representative sample of valid and authentic epithets: "exotic," "hybrid," "impossible," "tyrant," "visionary," "genius," and "important." Above all, "important"!

Whereas Balanchine and de Mille employed the ballet or ballet-tap mode that has all but disappeared from modern show dancing, Jack Cole developed an entirely personal mode of jazz-ethnic-ballet that prevails as the dominant look of and technique for dancing in today's musicals, films, nightclub revues, television commercials, and videos. Born out of his highly individual and innovative experiments with authentic Indian dances set to contemporary jazz and abetted with ethnic and black dance characteristics, Jack Cole's style stamped all his work with an unmistakable look that followers claim endures in the choreography of Jerome Robbins, Bob Fosse, Peter Gennaro, and Gower Champion, among others. Unlike Balanchine and de Mille, Cole maintained a lifelong allegiance to dance in the commercial sector, primarily the avenues of opportunity afforded by the Broadway musical, Hollywood films, and the nightclub circuit. That he was an uncompromising artist unencumbered by stereotypic artistic pretensions caused many contemporaries to dismiss his work as insignificant. That many of his musicals and films either flopped at the box office or passed rapidly into oblivion only added to the reservations critics expressed about his work and its value. Not that their suspicions were totally unfounded. How could a visionary artist of such staggering impact own a list of Broadway credits like *Allah Be Praised, Alive and Kicking, May Wine, Thumbs Up, Kean, Donnybrook, Mata Hari,* and *Chu Chin*? Unlike the director-choreographers who followed him, Cole accepted the risk and limitations of adapting

Jack Cole rehearses
dancers for the Harold
Arlen musical *Jamaica*,
1957. (*Photo: Theater
Collection, Free Library
of Philadelphia.*)

his dance contribution to the director's demands. He paid the price. The
overwhelming critical assessment varied little throughout his career; it
was always "lousy show but great dances." A major artistic vision cannot
succeed without major artistic control. Consequently, much of this body
of ground-breaking movement went into a nightclub act where Cole
controlled everything. When management, musical directors, or the
performance environment threatened that control, Cole and his dancers
walked out. However, under ideal (for him), conditions, the act
prospered and received flattering notices, like this one for an engagement
at New York's Rainbow Room:

> Now and then a footsore recorder of nocturnal rites discovers a performer
> who proved that night club entertainment really need not be so banal and
> repetitious, or rely permanently on the accepted cliché. In an orbit where
> dancing almost invariably means the noisy routines of the hard-working
> chorus girls, the soulful gyrations of ballroom duos or the epidermic display
> of the "interpretive" school, Jack Cole seems bent on doing something
> daring. Daring, because he is challenging the rudimentary taste of café
> habitués. With a quartet of young women and a male dancer, all of whom
> have appeared on the concert platform, he is trying to present dancing that
> has excitement for its original form and content without straining the
> mental capacity of a public conditioned by the tried-and-true formula. So
> far as we're concerned, it is still a question as to whether or not he has

overcome the innate suspicion of the average ringside guest against anything that is remotely esoteric—i.e., anything said average guest has not seen a thousand times before.

Though noticed, the dances went unrecorded—except in the kinetic memory and appreciation of the dancers and students who would go on to successful show business careers without him.

The word *difficult* describes Jack Cole best. Jack Cole the person? Difficult! Jack Cole the artist? Difficult! The Jack Cole technique? Difficult! Jack Cole made extraordinary demands on his dancers. He expected an outstanding technique, classical training, total dedication, ethnic dance study, exhaustive floor work, acrobatic flexibility, and meticulous isolations. Cole demanded everything and got it from his loyal, totally professional roster of dancers. He wasn't easy on them either, as he confided in *Dance Magazine,* January 1968:

> Sometimes you have to slap them. Sometimes you have to kiss them. It isn't like painting or writing or something that can be done in solitude. The trouble with choreography is you have to get the person out of the way before you can bring out the dancer.

Jack Cole began his career with Ruth St. Denis, Ted Shawn, and the Humphrey-Weidman dancers. His earliest exposure to oriental dance came from Ruth St. Denis, whose approach to East Indian dance amounted to the pious affectation involved in offering ritual dances on Buddha's birthday and later, devising for the stage theatrical if un-authentic Indian dances that, according to Cole, made her appear to be "goosing angels." Unlike his early mentor, Cole sought to absorb the dance vocabulary of *authentic* East Indian dance. After an appearance with the Denishawn Company in a Cambodian ballet, he began research at Columbia University into oriental history, culture, costumes, and dance that lasted a lifetime. He read the Bhagavad-Gita, studied East Indian dance with La Meri and Uday Shankar, and expanded his studies to include the American Indian, the black American, and the Caribbean and South American ethnic heritages.

Throughout his career, Cole viewed information, thought, and knowl-edge as necessary support systems to his life as a dancer and choreog-rapher, not merely as avenues to the period, style, and local-color prepa-ration for each new show. His personal dance library was said to be equal to if not superior to any in private hands. Firsthand observation com-

A lifelong exposure to oriental dance made Jack Cole the logical choice to choreograph the musical *Kismet*. (*Photo: Theater Collection, Free Library of Philadelphia.*)

plemented the fruits of erudition. Cole traveled widely in search of the details that made his work believably authentic. No continent or region proved too inaccessible—be it in the Middle East, the Caribbean, or South America. When a production called for less-than-authentic dance material, he researched anyway. Said he in the same article, "You can't satirize or otherwise distort a dance form without knowing it thoroughly." Not every quest for knowledge and truth brought desirable results. A six-week pilgrimage into the Amazon jungle to observe native dances and costumes amid the dangers of oppressive heat, man-eating tribes, and similarly inclined insects produced the following reminiscence:

> What did the natives wear? Dirty G-strings! How did they dance? A rotten shuffle! Oog-oog-unka! to the right. Oog-oog-unka! to the left. And for this I risked my neck?

The experience didn't deter Cole from subsequent research. As former dancer Florence Lessing said, "He had a very comprehensive view of what he wanted to do."

What Jack Cole did do was to assimilate the ethnic dance of the Orient, Latin America, and Harlem; absorb their natures into his own motor mechanism; and then transform hitherto-alien impulses into a strict, gaunt, physical, neurotic, virtuosic, and sensuous style as distinctive in kinetic intensity as it was impossible to categorize. As with Balanchine's choreography for the New York City Ballet, Cole's dances betrayed an interest in movement as movement. Dancers interested him as bodies of acute technical preparedness willing to risk a performance intensity akin to religious possession in order to execute the spectacular movement he devised for them. As a dancer, Cole possessed a spectacular technique, almost inhuman strength, endurance, and a magnetic performance personality. He demanded nothing less from his dancers. If the dances themselves revealed everything that needed to be seen then no execution short of perfection need be tolerated. That meant controlled command of the swift pace, dynamic reversals, and unusual isolations that marked his personal style. In addition, Cole himself was gifted with tremendous energy that friends likened to that of a "coiled spring," and his choreography reflects the need for dancers with similar dynamic reserves. Movement in a Cole dance might rush headlong in one direction only to reverse direction with equal energy, or it might spring straight up as if to break through the ceiling and then plunge straight down as if to break through the floor. As media for movement, earth and air were quite the same to him; each was to be attacked and mastered with ferocious abandon. The bent-knee positions that Cole derived from East Indian dance served the "coil" in Cole always ready to spring, the pelvis always ready to gyrate, and feet always ready to flagellate the floor. Then suddenly, unexpectedly, well-considered flowing movements or a well-timed pause would soften the violent, "heathenish," high-tension impact of the previously thrusting, pounding movement, leaving the audience limp in the aftermath of such a dynamic range of movement. Beneath the glossy, perfect, professional sheen of his dances raged the temperament critics deservedly described as "nervous," "violent," "fierce," "physical," and "animalistic."

The Jack Cole legacy survives in its most unadulterated form in the minds and muscle memories of the dancers he guided, prodded, tyrannized, employed, disciplined, educated, and loved. During his early Hollywood career, Cole trained soon-to-be-stars like Gwen Verdon, Rod Alexander, Carol Haney, and Matt Mattox. There, he subjected his disciples to daily classes designed to prepare them for any and all professional opportunities. In 1944, Columbia Pictures hired Jack Cole to create the first permanent dance ensemble for a film studio. He began with twelve dancers, rehearsed six hours daily, and within months repaid the foresight of the studio with the best-trained dance unit in motion pictures. The serious training paid off for the dancers, since each received

Jack Cole and dancers in one of the bent-knee positions derived from East Indian dance and assimilated into his choreographic style. (*Photo: Theater Collection, Free Library of Philadelphia.*)

a handsome salary under contract to Columbia, as well as those in the film audience who enjoyed superior dance production numbers. Cole probably deserved his reputation for being temperamental, demanding, merciless, and difficult—if not impossible. What must be understood is that he cared excessively for dancing and dancers, and those prepared to accept his ways and follow his lead would be rewarded with the most valuable and comprehensive dance training available at that time. The muscles of the body make all movement possible, and different dance modes employ different muscles. Ballet disciplines the legs and feet. Modern dance conditions the torso. East Indian dance focuses on isolations of the extremities. Cole's choreography favored intricate isolations, and their theatrical deployment needed precise execution if the dances were to be performed to the level of the choreographer's expectations. No easy matter. The Cole dancer Florence Lessing recalled that mastery of those isolations required "a great deal of concentration, of control. You need a lot of intelligence to do this. It's extremely difficult to master.

Jack Cole's assets as a dancer included a muscular body, spectacular technique, and incredible strength and endurance. (*Photo: Theater Collection, Free Library of Philadelphia.*)

So many parts of the body, so many muscles moving in opposition to each other, and each in isolation from the other!" To which Cole dancer Buzz Miller added, "Cole demanded a lot of isolations; for instance, in an East Indian dance, getting each finger to move quite separately, like a Buddha. All Cole's work was very isolated—very strong, very controlled, very cool. Even his and his dancers' eyes and eyebrows." Nor was the mastery of technique everything. For the Cole dancers, a strong technique became a means to an end. Cole tolerated only the best dancers and trained them mercilessly to make his dance material vibrate with life. The unending quest for perfection demanded that in addition to technique all dancers master those felt emotions, attitudes, thoughts, and details that crown the moving body with kinetic believability. Said Cole in his *Dance Magazine* article:

> In the theater you want to see real people doing real things, expressing valid emotions in an artistic, meaningful way, disclosing bits of insight that will transfix you and make you understand something about life, and about yourself.

Cole's dance training forced the dancers to reach within themselves and align their disciplined bodies with their deepest emotions and their truest selves. Although during training and rehearsals he employed questionable methods, like vulgar language and physical violence, his goal as an artist was to use dance to attune his people to what was most vital and real in life. For Cole, dance made the dancer more human. He continued:

I just try to touch the dancer at the center of his emotion. I try to remind him of what he is—a dancer, and actor, a real person. If you're ashamed of this or that emotion, you can't dance. You yourself may not behave a certain way as a person, but when you dance you must bring real emotion to whatever you're doing. Isn't that what dancing is about—emotion, life—and not just patterns in the air?

Among the pioneer choreographers who redirected the course of show dancing away from the influence and practices of the dance directors, Jack Cole and George Balanchine share the most striking similarities. In addition to sharing an uncompromising commitment to the art of dance, as did Agnes de Mille, each possessed the ultimate choreographic gift: the ability to devise movement so inventive, exciting, logically continuous, and physically appropriate to the dancers as to be as joyously danceable as technically demanding. Both were genuine innovators in that each achieved a true, permanent, and forward-looking change in the appearance, methods, and aims of dance in their respective domains. Like the Balanchine signature on *Apollo, Symphony in C,* and *Agon,* Cole's stamp on a work was so unmistakable that dancers and choreographers could always identify it as his by just looking at it. A good working definition for genius would be this: A person who achieves naturally what others cannot by all other means. George Balanchine and Jack Cole deserve to be called geniuses. Where they depart: One chose to abandon commercial dance, the other didn't.

The director-choreographers who dominate the modern world of show dancing owe their privilege and power to the three pioneer choreographers who bequeathed to them and us the following legacy: (1) a standard of serious artistry for popular show dancing, (2) a commitment to dance as an expressive medium, (3) a considerable expansion of the modes of dance to be used on stage, film, and video, (4) a new and more professionally important use of the dancers themselves, and (5) quality choreography for dancers to dance, for audiences to see, and for future choreographers to embrace as a standard for their work and a challenge to future expectations.

The Director-Choreographer: Early Masters

Once upon a time on Broadway the name of a dance director used to be printed in small type, down at the bottom of the program credits. But that was when Dad was a lecherous lad, out on the town for a look at those glorious girls, girls, girls. Today a dance director is called a choreographer and he runs the whole show, a fact that is made known to one and all by an editorial device called a "box."

Over at the Broadway, for example, heavy black lines catch the eye and set apart the following words on the program for *West Side Story*: "Entire production directed and choreographed by Jerome Robbins." At the 46th Street Theatre, the same legend states that Bob Fosse was responsible for all of the staging of *Redhead*. Starting Thursday, Michael Kidd's box will decorate *Destry Rides Again*, and on May 14, Robbins will add a second when Ethel Merman's *Gypsy* comes to town.

So wrote Emily Coleman, music and dance critic of *Newsweek* magazine, in the *New York Times Magazine* on April 19, 1959. That the modern musical show has evolved from a medium controlled by writers to a medium controlled by staging artists can be attributed to the Broadway phenomenon here described: The director-choreographer who directs the dialogue, stages the songs, and choreographs the dances. The unified musical show predisposed to artistry as well as movement demands an overseer with the background and talent to coordinate its disparate elements into the stylish, homogeneous and artistically seamless phenomenon modern audiences now accept as the norm in Broadway musical entertainments. For years, choreographers of the stature of Jack Cole and Agnes de Mille documented the practical and artistic liabilities of staging and choreography made secondary and serviceable to the other elements of a musical. Then, there appeared on the show-dancing scene a trio of talents—Robbins, Fosse, and Gower Champion—who were prepared to do something about those problems. What they did, and to critical and commercial success at that, was to redefine the role of movement in stage entertainments, magnify its importance, and reverse the chain of command that governed the various artists during the preparation of a musical show. Banished forever was the mindless aesthetics that enslaved dance to the colossal, opulent, and lavish needs of producer, star, or specialty act. This Alexander Woollcott review from the 1920s vividly describes such musical staging, and it suggests the purpose and the power that account for it:

> Down in the orchestra pit the violins chitter with excitement and the brasses blare. The spotlight turns white with expectation. Fifty beautiful girls in simple peasant costumes of satin and chiffon rush pell-mell onto the stage, all squealing simple peasant outcries of "Here she comes!" Fifty hussars in fatigue uniforms of ivory white and tomato bisque march on in columns of fours and kneel to express an emotion too strong for words. The lights swing to the gateway at the back and settle there. The house holds its breath. And on walks Marilyn Miller.

Once regarded as properly decorous "wallpaper," the staging and choreography chosen to set off the star attraction now became the star attractions themselves—the all-embracing force that took unto itself the music, drama, sets, costumes, lighting, and orchestrations that served its vision best. In the murky, competitive, and ego-infested waters of show business, control is less inherited or bestowed than fought for and won. The dance director follows, the choreographer adapts, but the director-choreographer leads, and that has made all the difference. In the successful line of musical shows from *West Side Story* through *Fiddler on the Roof* to *A Chorus Line*, the conception and execution of the show's content responded most to the vision of the staging artist to whom the producers surrendered artistic control. The most striking modern musicals embrace the artistic philosophy, system, and look of total theater. Did the director-choreographers respond to this phenomenon or help create it? What cannot be contested is this: Their background, skills, and overall approach to a musical show blended the movement, music, and language into a seamless whole greater in performance than the sum of its parts.

Practical benefits accompanied the rise of the director-choreographers. A powerful individual responsible for everything the audience is meant to experience can minimize the gaps in the material and in communication between writer-collaborators. Productions rehearsed in a single studio minimize the chance of artists working at cross-purposes. A single creative environment that brings together the actors, singers, and dancers serves the best interests of all. For dancers and dancing, however, the most visible and welcome accomplishment of the director-choreographer remains in broadening the quantity, scope, and importance of movement and dance in the finished product. Writing in *Newsweek* a decade after the advent of Robbins, Fosse, and Champion, Hubert Saal noted that:

> . . . dance remains the essence of the Broadway musical, perhaps the most ineffable of America's lively arts. Body English is an eloquent language all its own. It may only be heightened or stylized movement, or a means of changing pace, or a stageful of exuberant bodies displaying raw energy, but the excitement of Broadway rhythm is as strong as ever.
>
> No song could express the sexuality of Donna McKechnie shimmering her way through "Tick Tock" in *Company,* or the virility of Bobby Van gracefully tapping out love signals like a Morse code in *No, No, Nanette.* Hal Prince may have created the "new musical," but even he finds it hard to abandon the climactic punch of big production numbers. Of course, they're not the old-fashioned kind—arbitrary, coming from nowhere and going no place. The new breed of choreographers, following such ground breakers as Jerome Robbins, Agnes de Mille and Bob Fosse, has gone to great pains in their efforts to integrate dance into the plot.

As any performer will tell you, added importance to an art brings with it added opportunities for its artists. The repertory of successful shows devised by director-choreographers offers the modern show dancer aesthetic and financial rewards, particularly the opportunity to step out of the chorus as many of the dancers did in *Pippin*; longer runs that secured for dancers a measure of financial stability, and an increased number of paying jobs available in revival, summer stock, and touring packages of dance-oriented shows. In the recent past, plays dominated the summer theater circuit. With the exception of occasional appearances by a beloved star or television personality in a dramatic vehicle, the majority of summer theaters now offer recent musicals cast with the versatile dancers needed to make each show work. First-rate dancers have never been new to show business. In the past, however, their range was limited and their professional opportunities few. What the emergence of the director-choreographer has done for the show dancer is to usher in the best, most attractive, and lucrative era of show dancing in the history of American show business.

The shows themselves changed accordingly. Stories yielded to concept; dialogue gave way to dance. The Arthur Laurents book for *West Side Story* illustrates the point. Since Jerome Robbins chose to communicate with the audience through the physical expression of movement and gesture, language symbols so gave way to dance images that the book stands among the most concise and compact of major American musical shows. Since then, the musical has depended less on story or spoken dialogue than on song and dance, and the attendant devaluation of the book has not only inflated the importance of musical staging but demanded that director-choreographers intensify their level of inventiveness to meet their heightened professional responsibilities and audience expectation with appropriately exciting and expressive work.

As the director-choreographers revolutionized the modern musical show on paper, so too did they alter its appearance onstage. The modern musical *moves,* and by no means do dancers alone monopolize the movement. Everything moves—scenery, props, lighting equipment, and the entire cast. When successful, the production acquires a very up-to-date, jet-age look: fast, smooth, sleek, and dynamically designed. So entrenched had the look become by the 1980s that when Wilford Leach, the director of the Joseph Papp–produced and rock-star-cast revival of *The Pirates of Penzance* indicated that he "wanted to see the operetta a new way," the choreographer, Graciela Daniele, knew then that the show had to *move.* When a show moves well, a unity of style persists—blocking with musical staging, musical staging with choreography. The term "blocking" refers to the process of arranging the stage movement of performers—traditionally, the responsibility of the director. The term "musical staging" refers to the process of moving singers, dancers, and actors around the stage in a musical number, at one time the responsibility of the director or the dance director. The term "choreography" refers to the process of creating the composition, steps, movement, and dynamics that constitute a dance—the traditional responsibility of the choreographer. Generally, these functions remained exclusive during the era of the dance directors, overlapped occasionally with the pioneer choreographers, and merged completely with the director-choreographers. From performers they must draw the characterization, feeling, and motivated behavior that constitutes believable acting; on performers they must impose steps, patterns, and dynamics along with the expressive quality needed to master the dance and make it theatrically effective; and from all they must elicit masterful compliance with the musical staging that brings the acting, song, and dance into meaningful harmony. The persona of the director-choreographer must draw from an assortment of character types: dictator, friend, psychoanalyst, craftsman, technician, and teacher. To what end? Control. As *Newsweek* asserted in 1971, the evolution of dance in the American musical show has transformed the choreographer to a director-choreographer, that is, "from pawn to king." The realm as constituted allowed for three sovereigns: Jerome Robbins, Bob Fosse, and Gower Champion.

JEROME ROBBINS

Jerome Robbins: perfectionist, craftsman, talented, demanding, difficult. Jerome Robbins: the supreme architect of unerringly designed, expertly made theater dances from *On the Town* (1944) to *Fiddler on the Roof* (1964). Jerome Robbins: master of comedy—the complicated, swift, and amusing Mack Sennett ballet in *High Button Shoes*; master of violent, dramatic atmosphere—"The Rumble," *West Side Story* (1957); master of childlike fantasy—*Peter Pan* (1954); the vaudeville and burlesque idiom— *Gypsy* (1959); and warmth and nostalgia—*Fiddler on the Roof* (1964). For twenty years *the* indispensable director, director-choreographer, and show doctor on the commercial scene and the first successful director-choreographer to guide the commercial musical show in its journey from a writer's medium to a staging medium. A critical appraisal of his career in commercial show business, before he abandoned it for a professional life committed to ballet choreography and a position with the New York City Ballet, reveals startling innovations that we accept now as routine practice in the creation of modern musicals. Robbins assigned to dance a primary role in the development of a show's dramatic and theatrical content as early as *On the Town*. Realizing that the compromises needed to function in the collaborative bureaucracy of the musical comedy business would only corrupt his vision and dilute his contribution, Robbins began to codirect shows with George Abbott in the 1950s. In 1957 his work as director-choreographer for *West Side Story* so blended the drama, dance, music, decor, and performance into a seamless, homogeneous whole as to establish the movement-conceived musical as the wave of the future and elevate the position of director-choreographer to the status of "most vital constituent" in the evolution of the Broadway musical. Because of Jerome Robbins, the theory that choreographer

The Mack Sennett ballet from *High Button Shoes*, 1947, established Jerome Robbins as a master of comedy in dance. (*Photo: Theater Collection, Free Library of Philadelphia.*)

control over an entire production could induce a more integrated effort characterized by unity of material, purpose, and style became reality. Between *On the Town* ("That was my first musical and I had a lot to learn about staging dances") and *Fiddler on the Roof,* his last effort on Broadway, Robbins staged numbers in *High Button Shoes, Miss Liberty, Call Me Madam,* and *The King and I*; supervised *Funny Girl*; and directed *Bells Are Ringing*; in addition to working on shows cited previously. However, no show was more important than *West Side Story* and the innovations it launched.

Jerome Robbins conceived the show as a vehicle for the choreographic interpretation of its major elements. Onstage it played like a popular *ballet d'action* rendered in a vernacular movement vocabulary. It was the first musical to be conceived, directed, and choreographed by a single individual. If *Oklahoma!* demonstrated how serious an art form the song-and-dance musical might become, then *West Side Story* demonstrated how serious an art form the movement musical might become. Serious, artistic, and successful though it was, the real accomplishment of the show was to open up new and exciting possibilities for the way musicals could be prepared and presented. Not only did Jerome Robbins shift the priorities among song, drama, and dance that had previously remained exclusive if integrated elements, he also broke down the boundaries among them. In this new hybrid form, movement assimilated all the elements of a musical show. Whoever controlled the movement controlled the show. True, the content of *West Side Story* proved ideally suited to the driving, violent, rhythmic dancing that became the show's form and style, but that's how the show was conceived. Choreographers before Robbins allowed content to dictate form, but none had successfully added to the equation the *concept* that dictated the content that dictated the form. According to an interview in the *New York Times*, the idea for *West Side Story* began around 1948 when an actor friend of Mr. Robbins who had been cast in *Romeo and Juliet* asked the choreographer for some help. According to Robbins:

> I wondered, if I were acting, how I would go about it. When I began to see it in contemporary terms, it made sense. Romeo's passions are so extreme, so intense, so adolescent. It's all new and fresh. The love you're feeling is the greatest in the world. Death is nothing. The highest suicide rate is among adolescents. I became fascinated by the subject.

When completed, the show resembled less the dramatic vehicle committed to a linear path of development many had expected than some dark and foreboding nebula forever contracting and expanding in color, shape, and atmosphere until the final moment of dramatic and musical resolution that brings relief to the emotionally spent spectator.

Much of what is valuable and long-lived in Jerome Robbins's work for the commercial theater issues from personal experience, purposeful research, and lessons learned during work on individual shows. Extensive research into period, place, and social mores and styles precedes and accompanies his work on every show. He reads books, examines pictures, studies photographs, and whenever possible, goes out to see for himself whatever is needed to approach each show on its own terms. For *Billion Dollar Baby* he plunged into the history and atmosphere of the 1920s to provide the Charleston and dance marathon needed for the show. For *West Side Story*, Robbins engaged in extensive observation and dialogue with and briefings from actual teenage gang members who inhabited the fringes of Greenwich Village and the settlement houses of Spanish Harlem. A revealing description of the impressions gathered under these unusual and potentially dangerous circumstances appeared in *Cue* on July 11, 1957:

> Once, in Little Italy at a street festival, he found himself almost swept up in a rumble, as a group of leather-jacketed kids came swarming through the

crowded streets. "It was frightening," he said. "You could feel the tension so thick . . . I don't actually know why the whole thing didn't erupt. Later on, I sneaked up behind a knot of the kids and listened to them calmly discussing whether it was going to be necessary to kill another guy, or whether they could settle whatever the argument was by a fair fight between the leaders."

At a dance in Brooklyn, one gang was all decked out in its formal uniform—red plaid ties, red plaid cummerbunds, plain red shirts and socks—and another in short black coats with velvet collars, cuffs and pocket flaps. Though he's been dancing since he was a child, Robbins says, "I never saw dancing like that.

"It seemed as though someone had told each individual there, 'Go have a ball for yourself.' Everyone danced by himself—it was a floor full of soloists. Later, after watching a bit, you discovered that they started with a partner, but after four bars or so, everyone took off on his own. But, make no mistake—everyone knew what his partner was doing at any given moment. There was no cutting in.

"On the slow numbers," he continued, "it was just the opposite. The couples were pasted together and almost immediately went into a grind routine. But the boys played it real cool: they would try to anticipate the end of the number and would break and just walk off the floor a moment before the end.

"What impressed me most," he added, "was the sense they gave you of containing their own world. Not arrogance, exactly; but a crazy kind of confidence. And there was always a sense of tension. At dances, you got the impression they were trying to exorcise their own tensions."

So successfully had Jerome Robbins translated the immediacy of those experiences into the finished product that the *New York Times* critic called *West Side Story* "a profoundly moving show that is as ugly as the city jungles and also pathetic, tender and forgiving." When Jerome Robbins accepted the *Dance Magazine* Award in 1958, he expressed gratitude to the producers of *West Side Story* for granting him the eight weeks of rehearsal needed to carry out so ambitious a project.

An earlier incidence of successful research occurred during *The King and I,* in which the Robbins ballet "The Small House of Uncle Thomas" reveals considerable interaction between acknowledged historical information and personal creativity. The decision to stage a major ballet based on Harriet Beecher Stowe's *Uncle Tom's Cabin* grew out of the valid thematic determination to focus attention on the evils of slavery and mirror the predicament of a character in the show. To make the movement both unique and believable in its context, Robbins borrowed

Jerome Robbins borrowed idioms from oriental theater for "The Small House of Uncle
Thomas" ballet from Rodgers and Hammerstein's *The King and I* (1951). (*Photo: Courtesy
of Rodgers and Hammerstein.*)

idioms from the oriental theater like mime, masks, stylized movement,
and stylized gesture and then put them to the service of a functional
dance entertainment that remains even today as one of the glories of the
American musical theater. A review by Richard Philp in *Dance Magazine*
of a 1977 revival revealed some of the mechanical details used by the
choreographer:

> Tears are rippling fingers, silver threads dangled on sticks are rain, men
> dressed in black and kneeling on the floor become mountains, women
> holding branches become the forest. Simon Legree, dressed in the devil's
> costume, pursues the fleeing Eliza with a walk in which his arms and legs
> are exaggeratedly turned out; dogs, also in devil's masks, crawl ominously
> across the floor in the heat of chase. The Angel from Buddha, Eliza's
> protector, conveys the feeling of a benediction through gracefully turning
> hands, which define a circle, then spreading out in a gesture of peace and
> an offer of help.

For *Fiddler on the Roof,* Jerome Robbins researched and experienced
firsthand the customs and traditions of Jewish culture and used his
findings to influence every aspect of that show's creation and production.
In an article entitled "Broadway Dance" that appeared in *Dance
Magazine* in November 1974, Roger Copeland made this observation:

Jerome Robbins demonstrating a step for dancers in the film version of *West Side Story*, 1961. (*Photo: The Museum of Modern Art Film Still Archives.*)

Above all, Robbins's new style of musical revolves around a central metaphor, the sort of compact, self-summarizing image James Joyce called an "epiphany," woven into the fabric of the production like a Wagnerian leitmotif. Nowhere is this more apparent than in his work for *Fiddler on the Roof*. We usually think of a director as a sort of glorified traffic cop, making certain that actors don't run into one another, or at most someone who translates already existing music and dialogue from page to stage. Had anyone other than Robbins directed *Fiddler*, it would be logical to assume that the extraordinary "Tradition" sequences were conceived by the libretto writer, since they provide the soil from which everything else in the production grows.

But "Tradition" was, in fact, conceived by Robbins; he insisted upon its being created after listening to the author's original drafts.

Apparently, thorough and perceptive research reinforces personally derived insights and generates staging and choreography that is both appropriate to the internal needs of the characters dancing and the external demands of their situation. Dances so created imposed substantial burdens on the dancers, who must be able to look into themselves for the feelings, responses, and motivations of character as they execute flawlessly the poses, steps, gestures, and dance combinations needed to execute the choreography. Robbins has been known to engage in acting improvisations with his dancers in order to humanize them and provide them all with the answers to such vital questions as: "Who am I?"

"Where am I going?" "What do I feel?" and "Why?" Like Jack Cole, Robbins realized that the force of dance movement comes from within— from what the dancer finds deep in the self that will work for the character being danced. Such a coming to terms with self does not relieve the aspiring Robbins dancer of the need for the technical proficiency that comes with study, preparedness, and total commitment. When Robbins auditioned dancers for a 1970s revival of *West Side Story*, 1,200 men and women appeared at each of the final two calls. Robbins remembers:

> I explained to them that this is a very hard show technically. "Don't stay and embarrass yourselves," I told them. But they all stayed—and most floundered.

Those dancers who survived such intense scrutiny participated in the most consistently admirable show dancing to surface on the American scene from 1944 to 1964. Their physical and emotional investment must have been enormous, but so were the rewards.

BOB FOSSE

If Jerome Robbins chose to put movement to the service of dance, then Bob Fosse chooses to put movement to the service of *a* dance— the always polished, always entertaining dance number he adroitly inserts at optimum intervals within his productions. Dance numbers interest Fosse because the choreographer genuinely believes brevity in the dance statement to be best. When questioned in the November, 1975 *Dance Magazine* about the possibility of doing a long dance work, perhaps a ballet, he replied:

> One of my great fears with regard to this, . . . is that I don't know if I could sustain a dance work of any length. I think that whatever I do—whether it's good or bad—is best said in four or five minutes, maybe six; and about the maximum I've ever sustained a number was about seven minutes, in *Pippin*, when the boy is indoctrinated into sex. I don't know whether I can hold the stage longer than that!

If Jerome Robbins chose to maneuver his writers into creating ideal conditions for the organic development of dance material, then Bob Fosse chooses to manipulate or impose, tamper with, or otherwise reconstruct the contribution of writers in order to make the material serviceable to his staging and choreography. Most notable in this regard was the "incredible amount of change" he wrought in *Pippin* (1972), changes for which Fosse openly assumed responsibility, credit, or blame. Discussing the creation of *Pippin* with Laurie Johnston of the *New York Times,* he said, "I don't think you would recognize the original material that Stuart Ostrow [the producer] brought me a year ago." He continued:

> I warned everybody to be ready for a lot of changes but I haven't got the kind of mind to say ahead of time, "It's going to be this way when we're finished." I get involved in the material and the people. And I never enjoyed rehearsals so much or had such a great cast—they really swung with me.

In this case, Fosse received "great freedom" from the book writer, Roger O. Hirson, as well as Stuart Ostrow, the producer. From composer and lyricist Stephen Schwartz, Fosse received anger, recriminations, and a major Broadway battle. However, as Martin Gottfried has pointed out, *Pippin* established Fosse as a show business force. He had sufficient artistic confidence and muscle to weather the storm and re-create the material as he saw fit.

Unlike Robbins, who came to Broadway with a background of ballet dancing and choreography, Fosse came to Broadway from nightclubs, burlesque, and movies. Of his background, Fosse frankly admitted to the *New York Times* in 1959:

> I started when I was still at home in Chicago because my parents thought I was very humorous dancing around the house. At 13 I started earning money at it, which gave me a slight edge over my schoolmates. I got used to making money so I kept on with it. I did tap, ballet, tumbling, and any other kind of dancing. . . .
>
> I have taken more from old-time vaudeville than anything else, . . . I saw Joe Frisco and Pat Rooney, and I have frankly based many movements on Charlie Chaplin—the way he walks and the way he turns a corner. I used to see every vaudeville show that came to Chicago two or three times. When I was 17, I worked in strip joints—I was the thing between the strip acts. I also played in more legitimate theaters, in burlesque as a straight man, I have a real corny background.

If Robbins's background directed his talent and craft toward expressive movement, then Fosse's early exposure to the "do or die" entertainment values of the self-contained acts of vaudeville and burlesque led him toward a career of creating show-stopping numbers for audience approval. In Bob Fosse, American show dance found the champion and master of ultra-professional, flashy, show-biz entertainments that ticket buyers and prospective performers identify with the up-to-date Broadway and Hollywood musical. Wrote Roger Copeland in *Dance Magazine*:

Fosse's choreography made it perfectly clear that the Broadway musical had broken completely with the easy-going European operetta, reflecting instead the brassy, accelerated pace and noise level of urban life. That sort of achievement may sound more sociological than aesthetic, but the product was undeniably impressive.

The Bob Fosse career developed out of the prospects of a show business dancer who turned to choreography out of "self-defense" and then to direction and choreography out of a need and determination to be the boss.

THE RISE OF BOB FOSSE
(A Scenario in Two Scenes)

SCENE 1

Young Dancer. Slim. Blond. Eager to work. Auditions for top-notch choreographers. Turned down. Settles for work with less than the best. Awful material. So, dancer builds his own material. Brings it in. Asks: "What do you think?" Answer: "O.K." Dancer becomes choreographer.

SCENE 2

Successful choreographer gets work. Slim. Blond. Older. Eager for control. Shows top-notch dance material to the boss. It's compromise time. No control with compromise. So, choreographer becomes director-choreographer. Shows his stuff. Critical acclaim. Blockbuster box office. End of scenario.

The rise of Bob Fosse to preeminent status among director-choreographers worked to the advantage of the performers as well. During the Broadway run of the musical *Redhead* (1959), a reporter for the *New York Times* asked the star, Gwen Verdon, why a "dance man" served her performance better than a "song man" or a "word man"? She replied:

With a choreographer like Bob Fosse as director, there are many things he can give you to do—such as a movement which will suggest a feeling, even when you are playing a scene. A choreographer is never afraid to move you around, while most directors have their mind on keeping you where you will be heard. You have more freedom. Choreographers have a greater sense of the visual, the composition of a scene, the look of a scene. You don't have to depend on words all the time.

Both Fosse and Verdon agreed that an underlying respect for exhibitionism accounted for the success of their collaboration. For Verdon, dancing represented an exhibition of "energy," "feeling good," and playing before an audience "all the games I never got to play as a kid." To this, Fosse responded, "When you're working with someone like Gwen Verdon you like to have her show off. Dancing is in great part sheer exhibitionism. People like to see people do things."

Although Fosse discounts the notion of a "Fosse style," Fosse dancing achieves a distinctive look within the sleek, brassy, razzle-dazzle of the Fosse musical. Though outwardly akin to a combination of modern jazz

Bob Fosse's choreography for the film *Cabaret* demonstrated the ultraprofessional look audiences identify with the up-to-date musical. (*Photo: The Museum of Modern Art Film Still Archives.*)

dance and tap that is capable of assimilating elements of ballet, burlesque, and social dance, the Fosse idiom wears a decidedly urban look
built on the foundation of the gyrating body. Pelvic grinds, undulating
shoulders, backward leans, hip isolations, and turned-in feet subject to
a tremendous economy of movement describe the essence of that idiom.
Little room for aerial ethereality here. Everything is earthbound, physical, percussive, and sexy. Few choreographers on the commercial dance
scene celebrate the physical sexuality of male and female dancers as
much as Bob Fosse. Arlene Croce in *Going to the Dance* described the
look as "classic Fosse twitch and slink," that predictably convulsive,
writhing, and sensuous movement that accounts for his no-holds-barred
assault on audience sensibility. Fosse dancer Ann Reinking believes that
the Fosse repertory constitutes a "whole new way of moving" that
demands considerable skill from the dancer. "It requires severe controls
and extreme freedom. If you go for one and not the other, you're not
doing it right." To help them "do it right," Fosse provides his dancers
with the motivation behind the concept, situation, and steps he gives
them to perform. Said he, "I try to supply them with consistent images
of what the ultimate accomplishment should be . . . something the dancers can play and think about while performing."

Since Bob Fosse makes up his dances during rehearsals, working with
the choreographer on the dances amounts to an intensely creative and
sharing experience. Unlike some other director-choreographers who
begin with a fixed and predetermined concept, Fosse chooses to build
his dance material piece by piece, through the process of trial and error.
Speaking of the evolution of his method for creating musical dance
numbers in *After Dark*, June 1972:

> The most difficult thing for me—because I'm slightly shy and inhibited—was
> to get up in front of people and try to *create* for them. I mean, I was fine
> when I was alone in a room, with a mirror and a barre. But . . . to be stuck
> for an idea in front of forty people, all of whom are standing, waiting for
> you . . . I found that the most difficult thing of all.
>
> I finally got to the point where I'd say to myself: "I'm the *only* person
> here. I'm alone. And I'm just going to stand here until something comes to
> me." And you're always *compelled* to come up with something quickly.
> Otherwise they'll think you're untalented. That was my major problem; so
> for the first show I did, which was *Pajama Game* [1954] I was in a studio
> for about eight weeks before the dancers came in. I had every dance already
> worked out by then. I put them all on in about five days! I'd worked out
> every part by myself—just to avoid that sort of embarrassment. Then, as

things went on, I found that dancers *know* that's part of it, the waiting for ideas to come. So I don't have the problem anymore. I just love working with dancers now.

When the interviewer asked "How can a choreographer create musical comedy dance numbers, not knowing who or what will be in the chorus?" Fosse went on:

With *Pajama Game,* I worked thoroughly on detail. I still prepare. I give myself six weeks preparation in the studio before the dancers come into it. And that's also true for films. But now I only rough out the dances. I don't go into great detail. I've found that when dancers come in, their personalities or the way they do a step may lead me in a different direction than I'd originally planned. So I try to be much more flexible than formerly. You have to be fluid enough to adjust to the performers. If you're rigid and won't give in on something, it just never seems to work out right anyway.

Now, when I work in the studio, I go through each number and try to get a combination—or just a general feeling of what I want. Just eight bars of movement and I can build from that, with variations. And patterns. . . . Patterns were difficult for me to do in the beginning because they are so strange. I mean, sometimes a simple straight line is the most effective thing you can have.

Three years later, during the Broadway run of *Chicago* (1975), Fosse added these observations in an interview with Richard Philp in *Dance Magazine,* November 1975:

When the show is originally conceived, I usually do not have visual images of the choreography, other than some vague idea of excellence. As I talk about the show, small ideas occur to me. When working on the script, I start getting a few more ideas. And then I go into a studio all by myself, exactly six weeks before rehearsals begin. I've worked this way since my first show and it's become sort of a tradition. And I just hole up in there and spend hour after hour, reading the script and playing the score. And sometimes I just play music that's not even in the score.

I start various steps at one time or another, trying various combinations. About the fifth week, I call in a couple of assistants and try out on them what I've done.

I examine each piece and question it and question its lyric and just fool around with movement and hope. I usually keep a little notebook of odd ideas and *somehow* the dances start to formulate. I used to be able to create entire dances without the dancers. I could do it all on myself. But I've found as I've gotten older that I can't push myself that far, I can only do—oh, eight or sixteen bars of a dance alone, and then it emerges more when I have the dancers who are going to perform it.

For some reason, I find it difficult to choreograph sitting down. I have to know what the steps feel like, and thereby bring some originality to them, bring something personal to them. And even though I don't dance nearly as well as I used to, I still try to do all my choreography myself, at least in some form. Admittedly, sometimes I fall flat on my face in front of the dancers, and I say to them, "You're not supposed to do this, fall on your face; you're supposed to make it look graceful, but this sort of thing is what I'm after." I have to try it all. And I think I come up with better stuff when I do.

The capacity for honest, accurate self-assessment serves Fosse well. He confesses to not being an effective storyteller in dance as Agnes de Mille and Jerome Robbins undeniably are. Arlene Croce asserts that "Fosse knows his limitations, and he knows how to make them look like powerful artistic choices marked by daring and style." In addition, Fosse the choreographer does not put himself above taking suggestions from dancers. Addressing the free exchange of ideas among himself, Gwen Verdon, and Chita Rivera during rehearsals for *Chicago*, Fosse acknowledged in the same interview:

> They're both such, as I would say, *ideal* dancers—in other words, ideal instruments, like there's almost nothing you can't ask them to do that they can't come damn close to doing! They're valuable, as well, for their judgments and opinions.
>
> There's always three or four ways of doing something and sometimes I'd get slightly confused as to which way I liked best. So maybe I'd try one step, and then I'd try another, and then I'd not be sure, and they'd say: "Oh, keep this step, don't throw that one out, give us a chance to go rehearse it for a while and we'll show it to you tomorrow." You can see they're very, very helpful people. Actually, I can say that about all the dancers in the show.

When asked by Philp if he would take suggestions from dancers in the chorus, he replied:

> Oh, sure. I *have*. Sometimes the dancers come to me with steps, and sometimes I use 'em. Why, sometimes when I'm moving very fast, I'll say: "I want you to do something like this, and I want you to do it in twelve counts. Let me see something." And they'll do something. And I might say, "No, it's the wrong style. I has to be more so-and-so." It's all being general and they'll contribute. And, a lot of times, it's better than what I could do!

Although Bob Fosse discounts the notion of a "Fosse style," this number from *Dancin'* captures the earthbound and brassy angularity typical of his choreography. (*Photo: Martha Swope.*)

Obviously, Fosse respects his dancers and admits to his considerable good fortune in being able to work with the best. Predictably, the man can be most selective when auditioning dancers for a show. For *Dancin'* (1978), Fosse looked at nearly 2,000 singers and dancers; he cast fifteen. Talking about the joy of dancing in *Dancin'* for the *New York Times*:

> That's one thing I told the kids who showed up for the auditions for this show. If you don't really love to dance, I said, then you'd better not come back because this is really going to test your affection for it. You're going to be dancing more and harder than you've ever danced in your life. If you don't have dance in your soul, you're going to be very unhappy here.

Fosse's critics fault him for championing style over substance and for his persistent obsession with gloves, canes, derbies and other hats, and props that have become the Fosse trademark. Fosse continued:

> I've really tried to vary my choices to try to get rid of whatever it is that people call my style. And when you think about it, what are they talking about? Characteristics. I use a lot of hats, I suppose. But I started wearing hats because I started losing my hair. I'd wear one to a rehearsal and start doing tricks with it—so that became part of my "style."
>
> Also, I have bad posture. Look. A lot of my stuff comes out rounded over this way. And I don't have a natural turnout. In fact, I'm slightly turned in, so a lot of the steps I do are that way too. See? And the jerkiness of what they call my style is . . . well, I guess the jerkiness is just me.

Personal limitations account for Fosse's predilection for props as well.

I think I first used hats because, when I was very young, I began losing my hair. I thought, "Well, a hat will cover that up." So I became very adept at dancing with a hat on, taking it off, putting it on quickly, and so forth.

When Jerome Robbins abandoned commercial dance to pursue a career in choreography with the New York City Ballet, Bob Fosse took up the cause and argued the case for director-choreographers with shows like *Sweet Charity* (1966), *Pippin, Chicago,* and *Dancin'* and the films *Cabaret* (1972) and *All That Jazz.* Fosse's argument in *After Dark*, June 1972, makes sense:

> Musicals are more of one piece now, not scenes directed by one man and dance numbers staged by another. The ideal is to make the movement consistent throughout. To make the actors' movements blend with the dance movements. Again, as in becoming a choreographer, I think I have become a director in self-defense. I didn't like the way directors had the power to ruin my dances—or throw them out altogether. A director could say, "You've got to cut that!" Well, he was the boss, so I thought, "You've *got* to be the boss, if you want to protect the integrity of the work." Ideally the same man should be director *and* choreographer. . . .

The record shows how well Bob Fosse represented that ideal.

GOWER CHAMPION

Though not as personal as Bob Fosse's or as material-oriented as Jerome Robbins's, the Gower Champion stamp on staging and choreography issued from such a dynamic show-biz vision and craft that it sustained the old-fashioned musical comedy for two decades from *Bye Bye Birdie* (1960), *Carnival* (1961), *Hello, Dolly!* (1964), *I Do! I Do!* (1966), *The Happy Time* (1968), to *Mack and Mabel* (1974) and *42nd Street* (1980). Though drawn to material that never allowed him to break new ground, Champion's ideas and methods reflected the convictions of a director-choreographer. Although his reputation rested on the famous showstoppers that graced each and every production, Champion believed that musical staging and dance should enhance their onstage context and not be included for entertainment only. Late in his career, he told a *New York Times* interviewer:

Prior to his career as a director-choreographer, Gower Champion teamed with former wife Marge in MGM musicals like *Lovely To Look At,* 1952. (*Photo: The Museum of Modern Art Film Still Archives.*)

I use dancing to embellish, extend or enlarge upon an existing emotion. None of it could really stand alone. Being director and choreographer, the reason, for me, anyway, is control. If you do both, the style is the same; one concept that you try to fold in so there is a constant flow.

Like Robbins and Fosse, Champion understood the fundamental differences between direction and choreography when assigned to different artists in the preparation of a musical comedy. Traditionally, the director collaborates with the performers on the task of script analysis and drawing out the performance from the performers' mental, emotional, and physical resources. Traditionally, the choreographer designs and sets out every aspect of the dance on the performers, often in the manner of dictator, tyrant, or god. To his credit, Gower Champion stressed not the differences that separated the two functions but the commonality between them, which he called "musical staging." It was this concern for linking the acting and the dancing that accounted for the continuity in Gower Champion shows. With a visual conception or guiding metaphor of how a scene, dance, entrance, or exit should look, he would ask, draw, give, tell, or otherwise do whatever was needed to get the desired effect in performance. In effect, Gower Champion became a brilliant synthesizer, as this Leo Lerman review of *Carnival* for *Dance Magazine,* June 1961, pointed out:

The *Make A Wish* program read "Dances and Musical Ensembles by Gower Champion," seen here rehearsing the dancers of the ensemble. (*Photo: Theater Collection, Free Library of Philadelphia.*)

"Carnival Ballet" leads into Act I's finale. But this is not a ballet; it is more a montage of carnival impressions: tight-rope walkers, dancing girls, puppets, banner bearers, a grand parade, a ferris wheel, glittering lights and a heady atmosphere of tinsel and paint, Lili herself, and just about everyone else connected with the saddest-happiest carnival show playing the little lost villages and towns of southern Europe. Choreographically, the spectacular aspect of this "ballet" is the restraint with which technical dance has been handled. It never destroys the illusion—no extraneous ornamental lifts, no unnecessary quotations from the modern dance vocabulary, or even from the ballet dictionary. Everything happens on stage as precisely as it would happen in life, but brilliantly synthesized. . . . Vaudeville and social dance steps and sequences blend with marching, acrobatics and all sorts of carnival show routine acts. No person on stage ever walks or steps out of character. I was reminded of the kind of synthesis Fokine created for *Petrouchka*.

The achieve a distinctive and beautiful look in his choreography, Champion asked that his dancers transform themselves to fit his vision as well as such idiosyncrasies in his style as the "very tight torso," the tension in the arms, and the angular use of shoulders and knees harnessed to the demands of precise movement. The *42nd Street* principal Lee Roy Reams confessed: "When I'm on that stage, it's still me, but I have to wear his body."

Gower Champion took pride and joy in the pleasure he brought to audiences who found his dances delightfully accessible, the type of show dancing a person might imitate on the dance floor and feel it to be almost as sensational as it was in the theater. His high regard for that dancing compelled him to take serious, professional action to guarantee the exact nature of his contributions. The staging of *Bye Bye Birdie* was the first to be completely recorded in Labanotation.

Despite repeated successes, Gower Champion entertained no illusions about his importance as a choreographer. In a 1964 interview, he declared:

> I'm a musical-comedy dancer and choreographer. . . . The musical is my field. I create especially for the musical theater and I couldn't cross over to the City Center and do a ballet like Jerry can. . . .

When Gower Champion died in August 1980, Frank Rich writing in the *New York Times* offered this more positive and accurate appraisal:

> For all the commercial and critical success Mr. Champion achieved during his lifetime, perhaps he was never fully appreciated on his own terms. That may be because he was an anachronism. He was no innovator, like Jerome Robbins or Michael Bennett. He never created his own distinctive choreographic style, like Bob Fosse. He didn't try to tackle daring subjects, like Hal Prince. And yet Mr. Champion's body of work is as much a part of the history of the contemporary musical as that of his talented peers. By applying an unstoppable imagination, galvanizing enthusiasm and a taskmaster's professionalism to a series of unpretentious, empty-headed entertainments, he almost single-handedly kept alive the fabled traditions of Broadway's most glittery and innocent past.

The stylistically cohesive, artistically unified, and seamlessly flowing modern musical show issued from the collective efforts of the master director-choreographers. To these three talented, ambitious, and professional men did fate deed the responsibility to begin the transition within musical shows from the book as story, theme, and language to the book as music, dance, and spectacle. Because of them, the movement of the American musical theater became its material.

The State of the Art

Two director-choreographers dominate the modern Broadway musical. One is Michael Bennett; the other, Tommy Tune. Composer-lyricist Stephen Sondheim persists as a comparable force, but only as a writer going very much his own way in an activity that has become a director's medium.

MICHAEL BENNETT

Enter Michael Bennett. Choreographer for *A Joyful Noise, Henry Sweet Henry, Promises Promises, Company, Follies,* director-choreographer for *Seesaw, A Chorus Line, Ballroom,* and *Dreamgirls.* Profile: Begins dancing at age three; studies tap, ballet, modern, and ethnic dance; directs and choreographs student productions during high school; appears in community theater, serves as apprentice for touring stock company; at age eleven, brought to New York City for the first time. That memory lingers still: "I saw *Damn Yankees* with Gwen Verdon. There it all was, everything I wanted, a dancing career." Big break comes at fifteen. A stock production of *West Side Story* casts him in the role of Baby John; one year later, Jerome Robbins's European company cast him in the same role; returns to New York City the following year and dances on Broadway in *Subways Are for Sleeping, Here's Love,* and *Bajour*; teaches dance at June Taylor's School; becomes assistant choreographer to Ron Field; then, at twenty-three, gets the call to choreograph *A Joyful Noise* to critical acclaim and his first Tony Award nomination.

Although Bennett enjoyed dancing, particularly for his own pleasure,

A young Michael Bennett rehearses even younger dancers in his choreography for *Henry, Sweet Henry*, 1967. (*Photo: Theatre Collection, Free Library of Philadelphia.*)

he knew early on that his occupational goals were elsewhere. He admitted in an interview for *After Dark*, August 1975, "What I wanted to do, what I wanted to work at, was putting on big shows—not just dancing, but singing, acting, dancing shows, and I wanted to make these shows on other people, not on myself." Those objectives he achieved early in his career, so much so that in 1971, when Michael Bennett was just twenty-eight years old, Hubert Saal wrote in *Newsweek*:

> Michael Bennett, now that Jerome Robbins has deserted Broadway for ballet, is in a class by himself as a Broadway choreographer. He has the depth to plunge into the heart of a musical with penetrating ideas and the breadth to achieve his dramatic aims with a variety of dances.

Like Balanchine, Bennett thinks in terms of movement, and the expansion of dancing in the post-1970 musicals offered the environment and opportunity for a dance man to gain control and use dance to set the overriding look, feel, and tone of a musical show. For him, movement doesn't contribute to the development of a theatrical property so much as it *is* the development of that theatrical property. To appreciate *A Chorus Line* and *Dreamgirls* is to realize how much movement matters to this man. "Dance is the essence of the Broadway musical," he asserts, and everything in a Bennett show dances—the design elements as well as the dancers. In a 1985 *New York Times* interview, he said:

> What I do is very dependent on the design elements. Every time a number builds, there's a light change. Scenery can make or break a show. People think that "Dream Girls" has no set, but those revolving light towers are very important. They define the space; they tell you we're onstage or off-stage or we've moved or we are traveling. They are almost like the narrator. And then they start closing in. The dressing rooms get bigger but there are more pieces in them. There's more of a feeling that those girls are trapped by their success.

Still, it is the dancers that secure his allegiance. No other director-choreographer in the history of American show business has been as outspoken or effective in celebrating the skill and dedication of the hitherto unsung chorus dancers. Perhaps no one understands or appreciates more what a great dancer can do in a commercial context. Bennett's beliefs about great dancing mirror those of Jack Cole, and he speaks of them in a similarly ecstatic and mystical fashion. According to Bennett, dancers "can reach an emotional level, a point beyond technique, when they become part of the dance itself, like a fine singer going beyond the disciplines of training and practice and becoming part of the music."

The best show dance choreographers have always appreciated great dancing, but what sets Bennett apart from the others is his extraordinary ability to conceptualize the dances for his dancers within a commercial context and guide their evolution to preeminence on the stage. Bennett conceptualizes dances to support "the reality of a show." Since the reality of *Coco* was the haute couture of Paris fashion, the movement involved required the girls to be taught how to sit, stand, pose, make up, and wear clothes like models. They even spent an hour a day learning how to walk. The reality of *Company* rested on the friendship of a thirty-five-year-old bachelor with five married couples and its attendant atmosphere of suburban–upper East Side concerns; consequently, Bennett conceived the "Side by Side" choreography to make it look like "a show put on by the Scarsdale PTA." To prepare for *Coco,* Bennett went to Paris and spent three months watching Coco Chanel and immersing himself in the world of Paris fashion. The respective realities of *A*

Chorus Line and *Dreamgirls* proved far more accessible since both shows deal with the trials and travails of show business. Said Bennett, "I love show business. I know more about show business than I know about anything. I grew up in it."

If the Bennett career stands as a monument to dance as concept, then the best dances are those that are best thought out. For him, "the difference . . . between just a choreographer and a good choreographer was the amount of time spent thinking beforehand about what you want your dancing to say." As with the best writers and composers of the American musical stage, who dominated the scene in the 1940s and 1950s, Bennett, an example of the now-dominant choreographer-director, not only expected his work to say something but to *do* something as well. From a 1972 interview with Robert Wahls in the *Sunday Daily News*:

> My approach to everything in dancing is not in the step kick, step kick, back, change, step kick. That's not my bag. What I want to do is to make the movement give a psychological insight into a character, to advance the story and make a point quickly, as in a cartoon.

What dancing has to say and what dancing has to do determines for him how the material is to be played in terms of its relationship with the audience. Here, Bennett distinguishes between a "hot" musical and a "cool" musical. In essence, Bennett's "hot" musical is unabashedly presentational; the performers play directly to the audience or someone in the audience, as when the dancers play directly to the director Zach in *A Chorus Line*. The "hot" musical confronts the audience directly, as if to remind them throughout of the theatricality of the event. Bennett's "cool" musical approximates a musical theater version of the realistic play, in which the performers never acknowledge the audience and play out the show as if the audience could see it through the so-called illusion of the fourth wall. Bennett's *Ballroom* was just such a show. Perhaps the failure of *Ballroom* led him to conclude that "hot" theater is more exciting for a musical.

Unlike Bob Fosse, Michael Bennett begins work on a production by visualizing the entire show first and then moving on to its component parts. One of the reasons the workshop format worked so well for him in the development of *A Chorus Line* and *Dreamgirls* is that the additional time and experimentation allowed made it possible for Bennett to get a feel for the material and a sense of the overall tone of the show. The process takes time, and by self-admission, Bennett works slowly. Still, a concept so derived can set a unified style and tone for a show, particularly if the director-choreographer enjoys that singular gift that Doris Hering in *Dance Magazine*, January 1970, identified as the "precious ability to see everything in the abstract . . . to eliminate the purely pantomimic element of a given human situation and distill out its rhythmic and design qualities." Longtime assistant Bob Avian attributes the success of Bennett's work to the gift for accurate overall conception. Audiences connect with a Bennett show because of the particularized way he chooses to express universal situations, an opportunity that can only issue from a sound and special concept for a show. *A Chorus Line* illustrates the point, inasmuch as Bennett shaped and reinterpreted the input he received from his performers in the workshop stages. The dancers facing that audition on stage become a universal metaphor for all the crisis situations we have ever encountered, confronted, won, or lost. Yet, the materials of that metaphor spring from "one of a kind" individuals whose ideas, background, temperament, and personality separates one from the other. Apparently, the combination of universal values and individual expression goes far to secure audience allegiance if the professional situation allows a single individual to guide the show from conception to execution without interference, deterrence, or compromise. Understandably, Michael Bennett advocates the one-person-in-command situation, personally and artistically. As early in his career as 1972, he told a reporter for the *Sunday Daily News*:

> Directing came naturally, and I found out I liked to be the boss. I find it easier to get things done that way. If I work a year in a show and it fails, I find it easier to take the blame myself than to look for someone to blame or to feel that if I'd had my way. . . . That's way I founded Plum Productions. . . .

As might be expected from a dance-oriented sensibility entrusted with total responsibility for his dance-oriented shows, Bennett usually chooses to begin work on a show with a clear concept, but open to the results of improvisational movement and staging. From this, in an inversion of what had been the traditional method of creating a musical, follows dialogue. Like Jerome Robbins, he may experiment with improvisations to help dancers experience their material firsthand before setting the staging or choreography for that material.

When the time comes to choreograph, Bennett works from his body and not from his notes. In fact, Bennett claims that he never puts anything on paper because "I really don't know what I'm doing until I've danced it myself in front of a mirror." The emerging movement issues spontaneously, prompted perhaps by the rhythm or the melody interacting with his private image of what the dance must do. When the spectacular success of *A Chorus Line* required that he prepare three separate companies of the show, Bennett decided to work on the three productions simultaneously. The significance of the occasion to the interested observer rests in the director-choreographer's decision to allow *New York Times* writer Barbara Gelb to observe the procedure and record the progress of a Bennett rehearsal. The schedule called for rehearsals to last twelve hours a day, six days a week. Blocking considerations dominated the first days of rehearsal. Ensemble singing followed. Then, coaching focused on the featured singing of the solos, duets, trios, and quartets, and finally on the dialogue scenes. One must not assume that deferred dramatic coaching in the rehearsal process in any way minimizes Bennett's respect for the book, actors, or acting. In fact, he prefers to work on musicals that resemble plays—musicals with a story that have a beginning, middle, and end. If his methods depart from standard practice, it is only because his most successful work has been with dance and dancers. Nevertheless, Bennett assigns priority to believable acting in song, dance, and dialogue. Again, unorthodox theories and methods prevail, as with the style of "non-acting," characteristics of which include "natural" behavior and genuinely expressed emotion. In *A Chorus Line*, Cassie tells the director (and the audience) that "I'm a dancer. A dancer dances. All I need is the music and the mirror and the chance to dance for you." That situation sets up the perfect opportunity for the performer to be believable in the part, since Donna McKechnie and the long line of Cassies that followed *are* dancers playing the part of a dancer. Here, natural behavior begets believability with minimum effort from the performer and minimal demands on the audience. In a way, Bennett himself practices his system of nonacting through genuinely expressed emotion when he imbues each of his shows with an undercurrent of energy that flows naturally from his feelings about dancers, dancing, musicals in general, and Broadway in particular. Martin Gottfried, writing in the *New York Post*, picked up on Bennett's genuinely felt emotion expressed through the director-choreographer's powerful presence throughout *A Chorus Line*:

> The theatrical energy is his; the style and muscle are definitely his; but, most of all, the soul of it is his. Bennett's shows have many qualities particular

to him but the most striking one brings something back from traditional musicals that has been lacking in these concept musicals despite their overwhelming theatrical technique and electricity: that something is to use a much abused word, *love*.

As Bennett detects genuinely felt emotion in his performers, so do audiences detect genuinely felt emotion in Bennett. Although *A Chorus Line* was a collaborative effort, the program credit that read "directed, choreographed, and conceived by Michael Bennett" underscored what everyone associated with the production knew already: This is Michael Bennett's show. A less conventional but more accurate credit might have read, "From Bennett, with love." So emotional was the opening night audience at the off-Broadway opening at the Newman Theater that the audience rose to its feet at the beginning of the final number and applauded throughout until the very end. Obviously Bennett's deep respect for dancers and his concern for them as people makes the theory of nonacting work. For him, dancers truly in touch with themselves can become actors, and any director perceptive and caring enough to know a performer's personality should know where to apply the support and when to draw out the confidence. Willingly he accepts the responsibility accorded the father figure in order to become the loving manipulator he feels he must be. However, successful manipulators need control, a much-sought-after prize not easily won. Michael Bennett won control because he recognized the need to fight for it.

Once Bennett accepts a performer for face, body, dance ability, or personality, he invariably treats them with professional consideration and artistic respect. The preferred method is to subject his cast to public praise but private criticism—a well-adjusted attitude that respects performers as people. It's a practical way to work, too. Happy performers give. In 1975, Bennett revealed his method of directing actors and dancers to Sidney Fields of New York's *Daily News*:

> You don't demonstrate what you want from them. You let them go, just steer them, pull out of them what you see they have that fits your concepts of a show, so they can do it eight times a week. What you're doing is acknowledging their creativity too, so they become part of the whole show.

That Michael Bennett steers, challenges, and triumphs has opened up a brave new world of professional opportunities for dancers. In the May 8, 1978, *Village Voice,* Wendy Perron quoted long-time Bennett assistant Bob Avian on the subject of work for skilled dancers:

For years in stock and in a lot of musicals, whenever there were small roles to be given out, say three- or five-line parts, they never considered dancers. They thought all the girls had teeny little voices and all the boys were gay and they didn't want to give them any lines or any parts. They always went to the singers. Always. There'd be this Brunhilda of a singer and she'd get the lines as opposed to some beautiful girl in the chorus.

What turned the situation around was *A Chorus Line*, arguably the "world's biggest mass employer" of quality show dancers.

A CHORUS LINE

A Chorus Line exists because Michael Bennett wanted to do a show with dancers and the best way to begin was with the dancers themselves. On January 18, 1974, Bennett convened a group of twenty-two dancers, including himself, for a midnight session in a dance studio owned by "some Buddhists." They danced for a while, then sat around and talked at length about why they had started dancing, what they missed along the way, and why they wanted the life of a dancer. The session changed their lives. Then, when Joseph Papp of the New York Shakespeare Festival asked him to mount a revival of *Knickerbocker Holiday*, Bennett refused. However, if Papp could provide some time and space, an original idea for a musical might be pursued. Papp agreed to allow a workshop production. Bennett chose his cast even before a word or note had been written, and he set out to fashion a musical about dancers in a workshop for which everyone would be paid one hundred dollars a week. According to Bennett, "my agent freaked out," because in order to create *A Chorus Line*, the choreographer had to shelve a $1.5 million project entitled *Pin-ups*. Of course, what evolved from that workshop was a triumph unequaled not only in the history of American show dancing but a critical and popular success unparalleled in the old and distinguished tradition of the American musical theater. In June 1975, *Dance Magazine* published an article by Richard Philp entitled, "Michael Bennett and the Making of *A Chorus Line*." No better record exists for the genesis of this show. No better testament exists to the spirit that produced it:

Dancing in the chorus on Broadway can be "fun, messy, God knows it's hard . . . no promotions, no advancin'" and it may be more true today than ever that the "only chorus line you can depend on is the one at unemployment." "These bodies don't last forever," a dancer glumly quips. "Hell, I'm thirty. How many years do I have left to be a chorus cutie? Three? Four, if I have my eyes done?"

In one among many poignant moments in choreographer-director Michael Bennett's new musical *A Chorus Line* we are confronted with the difficult facts of a fiercely competitive and overpopulated career. People with successful careers intermingle them with life-styles, and it is the life-style of the professional Broadway chorus-line dancer which we have come to examine at the Newman Theater in producer Joseph Papp's complex of theaters on Lafayette Street in New York City.

The elegantly simple setting by Robin Wagner consists primarily of tall revolving mirrored panels at the back of the stage. When the lights first come up on the full company working on a new combination during (we are told) the final audition for an unnamed Broadway rah-rah boom-boom musical, we are thrust into a dazzling and umistakable dance setting, the studio, with its ceiling-to-floor reflections of every thing we're doing right—and wrong. The dance style is familiar to us all: long, diagonal thrusts, open palms, sloping shoulders which catch the not-so-subtle beat of Marvin Hamlisch's score and roll it back along the spine, snapped clean by the fillip of a pelvic thrust.

"Turn, turn," the director named Zach (actor Robert LuPone) calls out while dancing with and correcting the twenty-eight semi-finalists, "toe down, back step, brush, brush. . . ." Mostly, we recognize the unmistakably naked theatricality of the dancing, the over-stated lines borrowed from jazz and modern and ballet. ". . . pivot step, walk, walk, walk."

Twenty-eight dancers competing for a chorus which will have, in the director's words, "four and four—four boys, four girls." The bare economic fact settles with startling clarity: budgets are not concerned with broken hearts.

Twenty-eight dancers, multiplied by two, reflected in the glass wall backstage, and the effect is stunning. We may for a moment remember that twice again as many have been weeded out after yesterday's call-backs; we may recall that this visual swarm of dancing bodies was an economic possibility forty years ago, not an illusion created with lights and mirrors. But these thoughts are phantoms, shadows merely when braced against Bennett's brilliantly conceived opening number. "It's almost too good," Bennett says later that evening. "That opening is a tough spot to follow without creating a serious dip in the show's beat."

The audience applauds automatically, eagerly, responding to the instant recognition that it is going to be richly entertained—all of this and more on a wizard's budgetary shoestring in an off-Broadway house. And when the applause dies and we have settled back and look at those mirrors covering the back of the stage, we realize that we are also looking directly at ourselves.

Zach, the director, eliminates ten dancers, who leave the stage, their bowed postures communicating what we already know. Eighteen are left, and the winnowing job fills the next two hours, during which the director exhorts them to "talk about yourselves" and leads them through a rigorous marathon of dance routines. "This is a musical about dancers, like you," Zack replies. He is cool, direct, candid; he listens and he watches, he seems to understand; and finally we decide that he is not very nice—and will someday be very successful.

"Most of us," Bennett says after the show has been in previews two weeks, "do not end up being in life what we necessarily want to be. Most people are in the army, for example, or most people are in the chorus line because they have never bothered to open doors for themselves in order to choose what they really want to do. These kids," referring to the *Chorus Line* performers, "I've worked with most of them in shows in my choruses. I've known for years they were special. You can see what makes them good in their performances: feeling, emotion comes through. There's expression there. Some of the same technique that makes an actor makes a good dancer.

"I've been working about a year and a half on this." Bennett is credited with having "conceived" the show, while James Kirkwood and Nicholas Dante are credited with having written the book.

"I turned thirty and hadn't danced for about a year. As a dancer, I'd gotten in rotten shape, twenty-five pounds heavier than I am now. And I thought: 'What have I done? I've given up something that I love!' I wanted very much to do a show with dancers. I didn't want to deal any more with people who couldn't move, or who just moved 'well'; no, I wanted to do something on dancing. I started thinking about the days when my life was really the simplest—when I was very young and I was in the chorus, and I was very happy.

"I started wondering why I got out of dancing. And, then, what drove me to get into the business in the first place. What drives anybody to get into the business?

"I went to Joe Papp and I said I wanted a room, and time. And he gave that to me, which is wonderful. He wanted me to work up a show for the Beaumont, but I said no, I wanted to stay off-Broadway. I was much more interested in the show than in trying to sell it—without any stars!—to theater-party ladies, than going through all that and spending a lot of money. And I'm really glad I've had this opportunity to get out of that, uptown.

"So I got together with some dancers in a room for about four months and tried to figure out what had happened to us to get us where we are today. We talked, and I discovered that the things which drive people into this business are the same things which drive people into other professions. Although this show has a show-business setting, it is really about life, about each of us on the stage or in the audience.

"I like to talk about things, and I like to talk to people who talk, and so I determined to do a show—I had not decided whether or not it would be a musical—that really talked, not untheatrically, of course, because I'm a big believer in magic and fantasy."

Magic and fantasy, two common elements in the unfolding biographies of the on-stage auditioning chorus members. Through monologues and song, through dance, the characterizations are sharply drawn, as they would have to be when dealing with eighteen characters. To the credit of the performers, individuals emerge briefly, subtly, without upsetting the precariously beautiful ensemble work. Even Donna McKechnie (the show's star, if one is pressed to picking stars in a starless show) is carefully linked to the other anxious dancers. The character she plays, Cassie, is a still-young, formerly successful Broadway soloist who has hit on bad times and is now seeking the work she needs—any work, even in a corps. We learn that she also once lived with the director Zach, disastrously.

McKechnie is the only dancer given a solo on the empty stage (the others have taken a break, and it is only Zach who watches), performing in front of reflecting panels which at one point close in quickly around her in a semi-circle, like a trap. Because Cassie's past and talents have been given special focus, we are a bit more interested to find out whether she gets the job she wants and needs, or not.

"Donna and I work well together," Bennett says of the dancer he brought to prominence on Broadway with his choreography for *Promises, Promises* and *Company*. They've known one another since appearing together in the chorus of *Hullabaloo* on television, which Bennett feels is "an awfully long time ago. And," he observes, "we also dance very similarly. I mean, Donna's the only girl I know who dances as strong as a man without *any* tension. And yet the dancing she does is incredibly lyrical. She does me in!"

Bennett once said that he felt it necessary to play a father-role to members of his casts, which include (as choreographer, or as choreographer-director): *A Joyful Noise* (generally conceded to be a flop, with the exception of Bennett's choreography), *Henry, Sweet Henry* (again a question of a choreographer in search of a show), *Promises, Promises* (with McKechnie leading off the show-stopping "Turkey Lurkey" number), *Coco, Company, Follies, Twigs* (his first non-musical), *Seesaw* (which he was called in to save out-of-town from what would have been sure disaster), as well as some film work and a TV stint.

Does he see himself as the director, Zach, in *A Chorus Line*?

"I feel sorry for people who are judges. After all, who is he, to play God? I think that that's part of what the show's about. We all have to do that sort of thing at times. And you're never completely right. You can't be.

"Yes, there's a lot of me in Zach, but there's also a lot of me in the other characters, as well. Zach's pivotal. He serves structurally as a driving force; so, for the sake of the play, the audition is handled by him not necessarily the way I would handle an audition. But, because I'm a director directing a director, I have to pull from myself.

"A lot of times, in fact, the material in this show is based on things which have happened to members of the cast. They don't necessarily play their own material, though. Even though they're singing and dancing, and even though my staging makes use stylistically of heightened reality and internal monologue, the content of what they're saying is very real."

As each actor auditioning emerges briefly from the anonymity of the chorus line, we discover something about the making of a dancer. The experiences recalled are not unfamiliar; collectively, they belong to each of us and touch on deeply personal associations. One dancer was always "busy giving garage recitals" as a child, another forced to fill her mother's unfulfilled dream of becoming a ballerina; one gets hooked on *Red Shoes*, another is bounced from "method" classes at HSPA and takes up dance to compensate; others dance in nightclubs in Kansas City at age fifteen to make $60 per week or bus to the Big Apple from corn country to become a Rockette or land on stage at five years of age in *King and I*. One particularly notes Carole Bishop as Sheila in "At The Ballet," Ronald Dennis leading the company in a jazzy black routine, Renee Baughman and Don Percassi in a fast-paced comic number called "Sing!" For a while, the book plots the pain and confusion, the small victories and the promise of adolescence. Catch phrases and commonly held sentiments of the late 1950's and the '60's fly by like buckshot, stinging a bit as we're reminded too often for comfort that these kids competing on stage were born in 1952 or 1953 or 1955; and if they have trouble cutting it in a youth-oriented culture, then what's to become of us, the adults, sitting out here looking at ourselves in those damned mirrors?

Bennett's extraordinary skill and capacity for condensing his meaning to its essence makes this exposition compelling, funny and filled with bitter-sweet comment. Situations which in the telling might seem simply cliché are turned around on us in such a way that we feel comfortable learning again what we have known—that life is made up of combinations of clichés, like combinations of steps of chains or molecules. But Bennett's dancing barely ever stops, only now and then for breath.

"Choreography is not about steps, just steps, in terms of shows," Bennett remarks. "I like to think I make the best dances I can, but I'm also interested in dancing being right for a character. Most importantly, dancing has to continue the story line. And it's got to have a point of view. It's got to be about something. *That* I've never found just working with dancers in a room. You do it sitting somewhere and thinking about it. . . .

"After that, I do pre-production on the show with two or three dancers for a couple of months, working some things out before I'm finally faced with, say, twenty-seven dancers. But the real difference between just a choreographer and a good choreographer is your having thought through in the early stages what you want your dancing to say."

Bennett says that he has always tried to do every show differently, although he admits it is difficult to find a really new-looking step. What he seems concerned with most, from one show to the next, is the use of dance as an integral factor in creating the overall tone of the show, the use of theater dance as a parallel—not supplementary—contribution to the total effect. The concept is not new by any means, but it is seldom transferred from the conceptual to the working stages so successfully as it is in Bennett's more recent work.

Zach selects his eight dancers, and we are relieved that a decision has been made, even if we don't agree. The real conclusion, however, begins as the lights go up for the curtain calls. In another setting, with other material preceding, the slick show-biz step-kick top-hat prancing and smiling might have passed as a luscious plum; here, however, it becomes a devastating comment on the lives of youngsters longing after the glitter and the glamour of Broadway. After watching these dancers all evening long in their rehearsal clothes, they emerge in champagne-colored costumes of satiny material and spin a choreographic confection, subtly laced with gall and poison.

"I think step-kick is America's applause sign." Judging by the enthusiastic response, Bennett's barometer points to a truth about our continuing need to be entertained. "Choreographer after choreographer uses it," he continues, "and the audiences always burst into applause. It's conditioning."

Bennett meant the conclusion of *A Chorus Line* to be ". . . a comment on the audience, as well as on the state of dancing in musical-comedy theater. I want to end with this image. I want the audience to walk out of the theater saying, 'Those kids shouldn't be in a chorus!' And I want the people in that audience to go to other shows and think about what's really gone into making that chorus, I want them to ask: 'Who's behind that star? Who else is on stage?'

"And I want every chorus kid in the country to say, 'If those chorus kids can do it, maybe I can do it!'

"If just everybody had the guts to try harder, to push out, to do. . . ."

According to Joseph Papp, whose nonprofit New York Shakespeare Festival produced the play on Broadway:

There's something timeless about the show. It really is about Broadway, about the Broadway musical theater, which makes it kind of a perennial. *A Chorus Line* is Broadway, in a way. . . . My guess is that it can run forever.

Of course, it can't, and it won't. But when *A Chorus Line* registered performance number 3,389, making it the longest-running show in Broadway history, Michael Bennett celebrated the occasion by staging a performance among the most exciting ever recorded in the annals of the American theater. *New York Times* critic Frank Rich was there and published this "review" in 1983 in his "Critic's Notebook":

The only sad thing about a· great night in the theater is its evanescence. When it's over, it's over. You can remember the performance forever, of course. But you can't recreate that virgin sensation—that almost numbing exhilaration—of witnessing something new and different and exciting in the theater for the very first time.

So there was a lot of reminiscing Thursday night, when 1,472 friends of *A Chorus Line* gathered in Shubert Alley for a reception preceding the musical's record-breaking 3,389th performance. Strolling about, I heard the same conversation over and over. People were trying to reconstruct that electric night eight years ago when they first saw this show at the Public Theater before anyone knew that *A Chorus Line* might move to Broadway, let alone become the longest-running production of all time.

And implicit in these conversations was that sadness. While everyone was looking forward to having grand fun at the gala, everyone was also conceding, in advance, that the past could not be recaptured. Whatever happened inside the Shubert Theatre, once the curtain went up at 10:30, would still be second-best to that first, revelatory performance of years ago. Worse, no one could escape the fact that, however advanced *A Chorus Line* was for its time, that time was already part of history. The revolutions this musical wrought—in the way musicals are staged, produced and written—had long since been assimilated in hit musicals that followed. There were not surprises left, heaven knows, in the show's text. Pressed to the wall, some of the gathered might even have confessed a reluctance to hear yet another rendition of "What I Did for Love."

But two and a half hours later, as the same audience poured back into Shubert Alley, no one was jaded anymore, no one was talking about old memories. What people were saying, instead, is simply this: They had rarely, if ever, seen anything as exciting in a Broadway theater as the 3,389th performance of "A Chorus Line."

It is perhaps impossible to explain or understand all the factors that transformed a promotional event into a theatrical experience that was even more poignant than it was thrilling.

Some of the charge can be attributed to the good will that ran like a red-hot current through the house. When Michael Bennett said, "I love you, Joseph Papp," and embraced Mr. Papp on stage at the evening's end, it wasn't just show-biz sentimentality. Mr. Bennett is the foremost director in the big-money commercial theater; Mr. Papp is the foremost producer in the innovative nonprofit theater; as lines in the American theater are drawn, these men work opposite sides of the street. Yet neither Mr. Bennett's Broadway career nor Mr. Papp's Public Theater might have thrived if Mr. Papp hadn't given Mr. Bennett a home to develop *A Chorus Line* a decade ago. When the men embraced, it was the most palpable imaginable reminder that the best people in the American theater, whatever theatrical tastes they represent, share a common bond and goal.

But surely the most crucial factor in the evening by far was Mr. Bennett himself. This director is always a step ahead of the audience—and that proved to be true even when the audience was as knowing as the one that gathered Thursday night. Mr. Bennett's plan for the evening was to work every *Chorus Line* alumnus he could find into the performance. But Mr. Bennett—even with only three days of rehearsals—did not settle for just throwing an extra 300 bodies on stage. Rather, in a feat of artistry and logistics that boggles the mind, he gave us a new show that accomplished the seemingly impossible: He made us look at now overfamiliar material through fresh eyes.

Amazingly, this large new version did not jazz up *A Chorus Line*—it took the musical back to its intimate roots, to the emotions it aroused at the start. We were forced to remember that *A Chorus Line* is, simply, a show about those brave performers who insist on devoting their lives to the theater, even though the chances of fame, fortune and recognition are terribly slim. They are talented people who care about their work more than the rewards.

And they are performers who exist anywhere there is a stage. Among the ones at the Shubert were Chikae Ishikawa, who belted out "Nothing" in Japanese, and whole group of international *Chorus Line* alumni who performed the penultimate scene in the show in eleven languages simultaneously. That's the scene in which the dancers explain why they stick with the theater until their bodies can't take it anymore—a scene that, as performed by this polyglot assemblage, gave the ensuing "What I Did for Love" a literal universality that blotted out every previous version of the song.

But perhaps the most extraordinary of Mr. Bennett's touches came at the show's outset. The introductory number, "I Hope I Get It," was at first performed by the current New York company. But at the climax, when the dancers retreat into the blackness to fetch their resumes and publicity photos, Mr. Bennett, in a lightning-fast cinematic dissolve, replaced them with another cast. As this identically costumed new cast marched forward to the white line downstage, photos in front of their faces, a white banner dropped bearing the legend "The Original Company." And, as the audience gasped, that company lowered the photos—revealing the performers we hadn't seen in eight years. Some looked as we remembered them, some looked older and some, distressingly, we couldn't remember at all.

The effect was a reverse version of a legendary number in Mr. Bennett's 1971 musical *Follies*, in which a line of retired, middle-aged Ziegfeld Follies alumni were suddenly replaced by a mirror-image phalanx of chorus girls representing their younger, vanished selves. On Thursday night, the effect was chilling because it reminded us that the anonymous backstage stories dramatized in *A Chorus Line* are echoed in real life: Though many of the show's original cast members have successful careers, none of them became Broadway stars. What most of them did for *A Chorus Line* in 1975—and before and since—they did for love.

In this light, Thursday's *Playbill* was an amazing document. Like a program for a class reunion, it contained biographies of everyone in the show. Reading through it, one discovered that those *Chorus Line* alumni who are still dancing are still in the chorus—whether in the drag chorus of *La Cage aux Folles* or the feline zoo of *Cats*. Others run dancing schools, or make commercials, or are looking for work. Yet, as each *Chorus Line* alumnus passed through, it was plain to see that the assemblage's depth of talent, dedication and professionalism epitomize everything stirring that *A Chorus Line* and the theater that produced it stands for.

One could go on forever about individual performers. There were new faces like Kerry Casserly (who did a hilarious rendition of "Sing!") and Gordon Owens (whose dancing as Richie whipped up hysteria in "Hello Twelve, Hello Thirteen, Hello Love"). There was the familiar face of Donna McKechnie, whose lines as Cassie, the brilliant chorus dancer who can't graduate to stardom, took on greater resonance than ever. When Miss McKechnie convulsively danced her mirror number, the ring of mirrors lifted away to reveal ten other Cassies mirroring her steps.

There was also Sammy Williams, who originated the role of Paul, the Puerto Rican homosexual. As staged by Mr. Bennett, his confessional monologue became a group recitation—with ten Pauls forming a phalanx of lost men, like the Sharks in *West Side Story*, all sharing their unhappy youthful memories with one another in a tableau of minority solidarity and mutual support.

A little later, after Paul injured himself, Mr. Bennett replaced one *Chorus Line* company with another before our eyes, with a choreographed walk that seemed to fill the entire theater with ghosts of Broadway dancers past. And not long after that came the grand finale, the full-regalia version of "One," in which ranks of kicking dancers kept pouring from the aisles onto the stage. Even this number was in part a new dance devised by Mr. Bennett for the occasion.

By then, the audience was on its feet. Surrounding us at every turn were the dancers in their gold top hats, all singing and crying and kicking clear up to our ears. The theater seemed to shake. The cast and audience had become one, united in the at least momentary conviction that *A Chorus Line* was the best thing that had ever happened to any of us. People were screaming and, when the lights slowly dimmed to black, they were sobbing. They were sobbing because they were moved, and perhaps even more so because the show was over. The stage with the white line was soon empty again, as if nothing had ever happened.

Like those first performers down at the Public, the 3,389th Broadway performance of *A Chorus Line* can never be recaptured. But that was the only crushing part of this event, and it's a price that just must be paid for a night in the theater that its witnesses will remember for the rest of their lives.

A Chorus Line was an unusual show created in an unusual way. Unlike the musicals of the great period from *Oklahoma!* to *Fiddler on the Roof* that originated from text, music, and lyrics, followed by five or six weeks in rehearsal and six to eight weeks on the road in out-of-town tryouts, this show began with an idea attended by the luxury of six months to develop it. The model of meaningful work created under ideal circumstances set a precedent that has since become state-of-the-art procedure for the making of musicals. Once, the typical musical came to Broadway because a story-minded librettist got together with a composer and lyricist for a year, and they showed samples of their work to a producer who hired a director who hired the designers and commissioned the orchestrations during the six-to-eight weeks' rehearsal before going out of town to close, rewrite, fame, or fortune. Not any more. The workshop is in. In, mind you, not new. After the success of *Fiddler on the Roof,* the National Endowment for the Arts funded Jerome Robbins's American Lab Theater experiments with musical theater forms. The workshop lasted for a year and a half; no show ever emerged from the experiment. Speculation persists that Robbins adhered so faithfully to the old ways of making a musical that he missed the real advantage of the workshop situation: To begin a musical from scratch—without the book and score his generation would recognize as a "theatrical property." The "workshop according to Bennett" begins with an idea, allows the writers to write, be wrong and rewrite, provides the time and opportunity to see and hear the material on the performers and the option to abandon the project if it never really works out. What appears to be a luxury at first glance actually represents a practical and economical approach to the creative problems that beset the American musical. Bennett revealed these new guidelines for making musical theater and defended their usefulness in an interview with Don Shewey published in the *New York Times* in 1983:

> A workshop costs a hundredth of what it costs to do a Broadway show. *Dreamgirls,* which had four workshops, cost me about $150,000. The show cost $3.5 million to produce. Do you know how much easier it is to raise $150,000 to do a workshop? That means anybody with an idea for a musical could really employ a lot of out-of-work actors and could try things. It is, I think, the solution to the problem of the musical theater.
>
> It's one thing to have the script and have everybody believe in you and try to raise $3.5 million. It's another thing to have a show on its feet and to be able to say, "Do you like this? Would you like to be an investor?" The workshop process has enabled a lot of shows to be done that otherwise would be regarded as too risky or too dangerous.

Dreamgirls, Bennett's most recent Broadway success, also grew out of a workshop atmosphere, though its subject and its movement motif was the assimilation of black music and dance into the white pop environment and not, as in *Chorus Line,* a paean to stage dance. Unfortunately, the promise of the workshop idea must be modified by a recognition of

Michael Bennett acknowledges the audience after the 3,389th performance that made *A Chorus Line the* longest-running show in Broadway history. (*Photo: Martha Swope*)

some dangers inherent in that situation. For years, a growing concern has been voiced by critics and the public that deplores the demise of the well-written musical at the hands of the director-choreographers. Must the American musical theater be condemned to a future of style without substance? Of tricks without text? Of self-fulfilled song and dance? Will the omniscient and all-powerful director-choreographers who reject prepared material further discourage the already depleted ranks of writers for the Broadway musical?

Whatever the outcome, it can be assumed that Michael Bennett will continue to operate from the nerve center of the Broadway musical for years to come. When the Actors Fund wanted to bestow on him their Lifetime Achievement Award in 1983, Bennett's response was, "I don't want it. I'm only 40! This isn't my life's work yet."

We were all encouraged.

TOMMY TUNE

Ingenious. Unorthodox. Innovative. Unconventional. Original. Who else but director-choreographer-performer Tommy Tune, the latest sensation in the long line of director-choreographers who have come to dominate the Broadway scene? Unlike Robbins, Fosse, and Bennett, whose ideas and accomplishments pushed the musical show successfully into the future, Tommy Tune's achievement, as Ross Wetzsteon wrote, "is to infuse old forms with new feeling, to convert nostalgia into creative force, to give show biz back its good name."

The career of the man whose dreams were "of entertaining people in a Broadway show" began in Texas at age five when his amateur-ballroom-dancer parents enrolled their only son in a dance class. As his training progressed from tap and acrobatics to modern and jazz, ballet caught the fancy of the Texas boy who "just wanted to dance." Despite excellent ballet training and premature visions of becoming a great ballet star, Tommy Tune gravitated toward theater after the realization that a six-foot-six skinny guy in tights would never end up with the Swan queen. A road company performance of Rodgers and Hammerstein's *The King and I* was a revelation to him, with singing, acting, and dancing coming together into a coherent entertainment package. In high school, Tune extended his experience with musical comedy by staging student productions of shows like *Plain and Fancy, Damn Yankees* and *Once*

Upon a Mattress for the drama club. Determined to pursue an education in drama, Tune studied for two years at Lon Morris Junior College, transferred to the University of Texas at Austin, appeared in college productions, and had completed the requirements for a master's degree in theater except for the thesis project when the decision was made to leave the academic environment for the more professional ambience of Broadway. The day Tommy Tune arrived in New York City, he auditioned successfully for the touring company of *Irma La Douce,* after which followed parts in the Broadway musicals *Baker Street, A Joyful Noise,* and *How Now, Dow Jones,* the latter two choreographed by Michael Bennett. The Bennett connection proved to be an important one for Tommy Tune's career, because years later it would be Michael Bennett who would give him the big break in *Seesaw.* In what proved to be a successful attempt to doctor the ailing show in Detroit, Bennett cast Tune in the role of the choreographer David, a role ideally suited to Tommy's temperament and talent, and he trusted him enough to let him choreograph his own dances. The next big break came with Eve Merriam's *The Club.* Unable to work regularly as a performer after the Tony Award for best supporting actor in a musical for *Seesaw,* Tune turned to directing and delivered the quality work many felt accounted for the success of the production. A string of successes followed: *The Best Little Whorehouse in Texas, A Day in Hollywood/A Night in the Ukraine, Cloud 9, Nine,* and *My One and Only.* So did the Texas boy whose only desire was to dance become Broadway's triple threat.

Tommy Tune is truly unique. He is the only major American show business personality to combine successful careers as choreographer, director, and performer. Said he to Tom Topor in the *New York Post,* June 24, 1978, "I like to choreograph—and direct—but I like to lose myself on a stage as somebody else for two hours. That's terrific." He prefers to emphasize the similarities and relationships between his "jobs," noting that the experience of one feeds into his understanding and approach to the others:

> I've never patterned my life; it's always a surprise. I see that now I'm a director. . . . I'm not just the song-and-dance man anymore. But it's no big deal. I've been putting on shows since I was five years old.
>
> Directing is another perspective. When you're performing, you're the observed instead of the observer. Performing is the frightening thing. I'm glad I'm a performer because I have a sense of what it's like to be naked and scared up there, and I can step in and help them out.

I'll tell you, directing is like gardening. You put them in the ground, and you make sure they have sunshine, and you water them, and they grow.

One of the reasons he remembers *Seesaw* with such fondness and affection is that the experience provided the opportunity to balance the twin cravings for creativity and performance. In *Seesaw*, Tune played the role of a choreographer who dances, and he choreographed the dances of the show in which he appeared.

A few Tommy Tune observations on his role and duties as creator deserve critical attention. To Don Shewey, writing in the *Soho News*, Tune offered this self-assessment of his work on *A Day in Hollywood / A Night in the Ukraine*:

Casting was the hardest thing to do. After all, well, it was fun turning them loose, knowing when to shut up and when to jump in. A lot of directing is knowing when to shut up. It's quite different from being a choreographer. It's a much gentler thing and it requires a lot more concentration, more than just visual.

What's the moral? I don't know. Getting in touch with the soul? Maybe. Because in essence what we have to offer in the theater is humanity. It's humans, in living 3-D. And that means getting through to the heart and soul and helping an actor to let that come out of the eyes. Choreographers are much bossier than a director can be. The choreographer in me can be quite bossy; the director has to coax. You can't demand that somebody cry. You can demand that they hit second position with the toe pointed on the count of seven. It's exact, and acting isn't.

To Tom Topor, Tune explained:

Musical staging is real tricky. The thing I found out is that every time you approach a number, it's like starting from scratch. The thing we wanted to keep was the heart of the piece. You can take any show, you can slick it up, you can get rid of all the flaws and have it real smooth, and you have nothing left except the craft.

Where does he get ideas for his numbers? One favored technique is to work from images he allows to dance in his head.

I like to get an image in my head of something—just about anything—the "slow gait" of a five-gaited horse, a giraffe running over a plain, a rubber band being stretched—and I let the image work through the rest of my body.

At other times, the material itself suggests a choreographic solution. Recalling how he worked out the movement for the "It's Not Where You Start (but where you finish . . . and you're gonna finish on top)" number from *Seesaw*—in which he appeared in a clown outfit and danced with balloons an elongated, lyrical Marx Brothers routine (Walter Kerr in the *New York Times* described it as "Maybe the nuttiest—and maybe the just plain funniest number I have ever seen in a musical")—Tune described the following mental process that led to a showstopper danced in wooden clogs down a staircase into a world of three hundred balloons:

> What can I do with the metaphor? Top, top, up, up. . . . What goes up? Top hats. . . . We'll use top hats. . . . What else goes up? Elevators. . . . Airplanes. . . . But we can't afford elevators or airplanes. What's cheap and goes up? Balloons!"

If Tommy Tune's stated objective with a show is to "make it get to the audience," how does he test the product in rehearsal? To Ross Wetzsteon in the *Saturday Review* of May 1982 Tommy Tune revealed this little secret:

> Once I think the show is all together I sit through it twice or more. The first time I slouch back in my seat and close my eyes and just listen to it as if it were on the radio. If it passes that test, if it gets me on just a verbal level, then I sit through it one more time, only this time I stuff up my ears and watch it without sound, to see if it gets to me on a *visual* level. When the two levels come together, I know we're ready.

The director-choreographer is the real star of the modern musical, and no two stars have brightened the Broadway sky in the last ten years as have Michael Bennett and Tommy Tune.

Movement is alive and well on Broadway.

PEOPLE, IDEAS, AND PRACTICES

8

Show Dancers: Past and Present

They are called gypsies, though many among them disapprove of the name and its associations. They are dancers—rigorously trained bodies specifically attuned and purposefully acclimated to the world of commercial dance. They work on Broadway, in films, television, and video, usually in the chorus. They are among the most talented, dedicated, indispensable, and underpaid of America's popular show business artists. For no other collaborative component of a musical show have the nature, standards, and training of its practitioners changed so drastically as they have with show dancing and dancers during this century. Itemize the differences. Nature: then—pretty, agreeable young girls comply eagerly with expected assimilation into a faceless chorus; now—attractive, athletic men and women with a heightened sense of self and eager to be spotted for unique qualities compete for opportunities to embody a director-choreographer's theatrical vision, or at least be matched to suitable dance material. Standards: then—young, pretty and willing to learn; now—professional, versatile, and adept at adapting to a broad range of technical, dramatic, and theatrical styles. Training: then—some preferred but none required; now—a solid foundation in ballet, with experiences in jazz, tap, modern, ethnic, and ballroom expected. Usefulness: then—willingness to dance as wallpaper, in the sense of providing a pleasant background for specialty dancers and star turns; now—a determination to function effectively in the movement-oriented precincts of modern show business.

Women dominated the dancing ensembles of early-twentieth-century show business, particularly in lines of chorus girls devoted exclusively to precision routines. Fifty years ago, audiences applauded the Tiller *Girls,* or the Chester Hale *Girls,* or the Albertina Rasch *Girls.* For

139

The show dance sequences in *Staying Alive,* 1983, featured attractive, athletic men and women. (*Photo: The Museum of Modern Art Film Still Archives.*)

variety, the dance directors cast *girls* known as peaches, ponies, and show girls. Prevailing show business wisdom exhorted producers to "bring on the *girls.*" Most complied. Florenz Ziegfeld, master of the revue idiom and producer extraordinaire, glorified the American girl. For him the Ziegfeld Follies became a showcase for the chorus girl blessed with beauty, like the featured dancers Marilyn Miller, Ann Pennington, and Evelyn Law who dominated show dancing in early musical comedy and revue. His featured showgirls like Marion Davies, Mae Murray, and Nita Naldi went on to fame in the movies and other, more questionable, delights. In a 1925 article for the *Morning Telegraph* Ziegfeld himself outlined the standards for a Ziegfeld girl:

> Beauty, of course, is the most important requirement and the paramount asset of the applicant. When I say that, I mean beauty of face, form, charm and manner, personal magnetism, individuality, grace and poise. These are details that must always be settled before the applicant has demonstrated her ability either to sing or dance. It is not easy to pass the test that qualifies a girl for membership in a Ziegfeld production, but I am frank to say that once she has done so, much of the element of doubt is removed so far as the future success of her career before the footlights is concerned.

There is a prevalent impression that once a girl is enlisted under the Ziegfeld standard, her troubles are over and her hard work is ended. What a mistake! Let us hope that for many it does mean the end of trouble so far as earning a livelihood is concerned, that it means happy and comfortable home living honestly earned. But there are other troubles ahead for her, and plenty of hard work.

A Ziegfeld production is no place for a drone or an idler. Often are the times when you who read these words are just opening your eyes in the morning or are enjoying your breakfast and the early news of the day, that the girls of a Ziegfeld production are busy as bees on the stage of an empty theatre, if indeed they have not already put in an hour or more in striving to come nearer to perfection in that which is expected of them before the footlights. Yes, there is plenty of hard work for them in addition to that which they do when they appear, smiling and happy, when the curtain goes up. Giving a performance is the least of their worries.

How little the public realizes what a girl must go through before she finally appears before the spotlight that is thrown upon the stage. How few there are who succeed from the many who seek this method of earning a livelihood. And, I may add, from what totally unexpected sources come many of those who from the comparatively modest beginning in the chorus rise to the heights of really great achievement in the theatrical profession. I venture the assertion that there is not one honest, wholesome walk of life from which they have not come to some one of the numerous Ziegfeld productions. The society girl, tired of that life, the school teacher wearied with the duties of her daily grind, the one whose life has heretofore been devoid of purpose, the stenographer, cashier or even the waitress. Maybe she is a chamber maid, but if she has the necessary talent and qualities a place awaits her in the Ziegfeld ranks.

Let us grant that a girl qualifies for one of my productions. It is interesting to note what follows. First, it is clearly outlined to her what she is expected to do. She may be impressed at the outset that the impossible is required, but honest application and heroic perseverance on her part plus skillful and encouraging direction by experts very seldom fail to achieve the desired results. But it is only through constant, faithful endeavor by the girl herself that the goal eventually is reached.

It is not the work of a fortnight, a month or several months to train these girls for the work expected of them. It is the task of several months and it is a fact that a girl, either while rehearsing or actually playing, may be training for some character or feature in some future production not yet definitely fixed even in my own mind. Of course, she is also doing this without knowledge herself of the fact. To illustrate what I mean, an apt dancer may be in thorough unison with the others in that particular group, and at the same time reveal a difference in dancing temperament, rhythm or technique; she may phrase, accentuate or actually interpret differently. Not only may she unconsciously register a favorable impression with my associates and me, but she may also suggest something by her work that will lead to some new and novel feature in a forthcoming production.

Not much changed during the 1930s. The executive secretary of the Chorus Equity Association, Dorothy Bryant, pictured the Broadway dancer of 1937 as a young woman who works hard for meager pay, a female dancer far removed from the press agent stereotype of orchid-donning femmes fatales with mink coats and Park Avenue apartments. Her assessment of the realities of chorus girl employment follows. Note the premium placed on youth:

> Most chorus girls come in at the age of seventeen or eighteen. If they look more than twenty-five, whether they are or not, they're through. It's no field for the college graduate, because she has not finished school until she's twenty-one. By that time high school girls have already had experience on the stage. And there's nothing in a college education that's going to help you.
>
> The requirements for a chorus girl are much harder now. It is very unusual for a girl to get a job without some kind of experience in a dancing school or singing school. Of course, the exceptionally beautiful girl may always get a job.

Not so today. Show dancing distributes its opportunities to men and women alike. Youth can be an asset—but only if accompanied by ability. As with careers in ballet companies, show dance today profits from the increased acceptability in American life of dance careers for men. No longer does the serious and committed male dancer arouse suspicion, condescension, or overt or veiled abuse. So liberated, the male body on stage becomes as free to soar, spin, and pose as that of his female counterpart. The chorus boy now accompanies the chorus girl; the sexually balanced chorus reflects a more recognizable vision of dancing. At last!

As the profession opened up to all, so too did its practitioners progress from corpulent beauties to sleek and well-trained bodies. The earliest chorus girls of burlesque, spectacle, and extravaganza were a hefty lot. The beauties who populated the Niblo's Garden spectacles in the era of *The Black Crook* weighed a well-proportioned 150 pounds or more, with forty- to forty-five-inch chest measurements supported by twenty-five to twenty-eight inches around the thigh. At the turn of the

My One and Only gave Tommy Tune the opportunity to balance his twin cravings for creativity and performance. (*Photo: Martha Swope*)

century, the Floradora Sextet set the standard for the Broadway chorus girl. They weighed around 135 pounds, had twenty-five-inch waists and forty-three-inch hips. In 1927 the desired norm for chorus girls was a height of five feet three inches and weight in the range of 130 pounds or less. By 1934 the average dimensions of working chorus girls read: weight, 115 to 120 pounds; height, five feet four to five feet seven; bust, thirty-four inches; waist, twenty-five to twenty-six inches; and hips, thirty-five inches. During the late 1930s, choreographers sought out dancers, not merely flesh. Cattle calls gave way to genuine, rigorous auditions, with serious applicants expected to demonstrate technical ability in a variety of dance idioms in addition to a physical appearance appropriate for the specific show. As rapidly escalating costs reduced the total number of performers a producer would hire, the opportunities that did exist demanded multitalented performers who could do it all and do it well. The day of "just a pretty face" was gone. The day of ideal measurements was gone. Most dance auditions of the 1950s required ballet as well as tap and modern; consequently, the average chorus dancer needed anywhere from two to five years of training before seriously auditioning for a big-time show. To hope to be chosen for ensemble work today, a dancer must compete against hundreds of equally trained performers who take dance class regularly, pursue acting and singing skills, and devote considerable time to the selling of the total self as a

In the original production of *Show Boat* (1927), Charles Winninger appeared with a chorus whose physical norm was a height of 5 feet 3 inches and weight in the range of 130 pounds or less. (*Photo: Courtesy of Rodgers and Hammerstein*)

desirable show business commodity. Dancers who cannot sing or act become among the first to be eliminated at a Broadway audition. Because actor-singer-dancers can be employed effectively at any time during a production, their availability presents the director-choreographer with the opportunity to establish and exploit a consistently peopled stage world free from the fragmented effect achieved by the "exit actors, enter singers," or "exit singers, enter dancers," or similar practices of the not-too-distant past.

Modern show business makes extraordinary technical and stylistic demands on the commercial dancer. In addition to mastery of a wide range of dance idioms, the dancer must adapt quickly to the look of choreography that can range from period style to the movement idiosyncrasies of the choreographer. Most experienced and well-trained dancers can negotiate steps. What appeals most to the choreographers, however, is the ability of those few who understand the special "essence" of the step—why it is there and what it can do through its performance. The best dancers make themselves part of the dance, not merely executors of its steps. When casting *Cats,* the choreographer Gillian Lynne looked for technically secure dancers with "a certain kind of imagination . . . people who could pick up the vibes about what it's like to be a cat when you dance." The best dancers draw out of themselves qualities unique to them that color their dancing with an excitement that goes beyond technical mastery. Choreographers value the dancer who delights in the expression of a total self in movement, a kinesthetic ebullience rooted in the dancer's peculiar physicality that projects equally to fellow dancers on the stage and outward into the orchestra and balcony. The best dancers meet these ever-increasing physical demands of staging and choreography with the appearance of effortlessness, a property that has come to mean the ability to conceal the energy needed to perform the dance properly. Only perfect control by dancers over their instrument produces that exhilarating freedom and abandon. A dancer's singing or acting deficiencies may be corrected by a sound designer or some diverting stage business, but an error in the execution of choreography can prove fatal to a dance, a show, or a career. Consequently, modern show dancers recognize the importance of dance class to sustaining techniques and control. Viola Hegyi Swisher in *Dance Magazine*, January 1968, quoted Barrie Chase on this subject:

> While I was a chorus dancer, I neglected going to class. Now, if you don't go to class your technique deteriorates. You think you'll be able to call upon it when you need to, but after a while you'll find it pretty much gone.
>
> To ease your artistic conscience, the next joke you play on yourself is to assume the attitude that technique isn't important. You think of all the ballet companies whose female dancers work with a partner as if he were a ballet *barre* and you use the boredom you feel about those technical displays

Premier show dancer Gwen Verdon as she appeared in the original 1966 production of *Sweet Charity*. (*Photo: Theater Collection, Free Library of Philadelphia.*)

to put down technique altogether. That's how you may comfort yourself for your own loss of it.

Nor does the need for class decline with age, experience, or success. Premier show dancer Gwen Verdon advised:

> From thirty-five on, you take a class and workout every single day. At my age . . . if I take a five-minute break, I'm out of condition.
>   It's so painful to get back in condition. In a week, I lose muscle tone. Even if you are not fat, you feel fat. If you've danced long enough, you just cannot quit or you'll develop all sorts of ailments.

Dancers who commit themselves to show dancing today know that they elect a highly skilled, no-nonsense, ultracompetitive profession. For a major show like *Cats* the choreographer saw over 1,500 applicants on the way to a cast of twenty-six performers.

What's it like to be a working show dancer? When the show's a hit and the dances are good, the feeling is exhilarating, the work is fun, and the future appears to be bright. For the majority, however, the supply of qualified dancers far outdistances the demand for their services in major productions. Those who persist ride a carousel of auditions, study, other auditions, further study, further auditions, and so on. The show dancer must deal with rejection. Professionalism, if not maturity, demands that there be no rancor, unnecessary fatalism, or the advocacy of defense mechanisms that might justify personal weaknesses, lack of ability, or other liabilities. The instrument of rejection has a name. It is called an *audition*.

Are there a dozen show dancers alive who like to audition? Six? Any? Who enjoys marketing a personality that moves well day after day? Who enjoys bucking the odds every time out? Who delights in being judged by those you cannot see? Those who can handle auditions, or even excel at them, do so by virtue of unflagging mental, physical, and practical preparation. It was not always so.

In the 1930s, when George White auditioned chorus girls for a succession of George White's Scandals, over 4,000 girls with some claim to beauty or dancing skill would file into the New Amsterdam Theatre. Four hundred would be called back and sixty chosen for a forthcoming production. Though a dancer himself, George White chose his chorines primarily for their appearance. Specialty acts with spectacular routines provided the dancing. A contemporary newspaper account documents the atmosphere, objectives, and predilections of a George White audition.

> There is an air of almost churchly quiet in the theater at a call. The auditorium, not the stage, is full of the girls, the stage is illuminated by one light hung above it, and the vast empty spaces of the theater, the cavernous depths of the stage, are emphasized by the limited lighting arrangements.
>
> The air of sedateness is carried to its fullest extent at a White call. The stage furniture includes the light and one table and chair. Lending emphasis to the hushed atmosphere, George White conducts his calls alone. Seated at his desk in the center, addressing the girls he wants to see in soft-spoken questions, he becomes more the professor than the producer.
>
> . . . He is a strange sort of teacher. His entrance onstage to begin his picking is a quick, short-step walk. As he crosses to his desk his feet tap out a hoofer's rhythm. He still wears taps on his shoes. His small, neat figure wears the invariable blue serge suit, white shirt and bow tie.
>
> He walks crisply, tap, tap to the desk and immediately beings assembling in front of him his lists of girls. White employs a star system. Calling a girl out of line, he watches her walk to his desk, tells her to turn around and enters her name on his list, marking after it one, two or three stars.
>
> In his own words, "One star means passable, two okay and three a knockout. Girls is girls, always will be. Only the hair dressing and the dress styles change. I have no strict set of rules for picking the dancers. I just look, call them back another day and continue to look until I am satisfied with what I have. There are a number of things you can't have, of course, and I try to keep them about five feet five to eight inches high, and east and west in proportion. They weigh about 118 pounds. Hair doesn't matter, although I usually find myself with more blondes than brunettes.

During the 1940s, a Robert Alton audition for a Broadway show attracted 500 girls from which eight were chosen. Prior to the dance tryout, Alton checked the applicants for grooming, hair style, and makeup. An Alton dancer had to make a lovely appearance onstage. If a girl bit her nails, he rejected her. If a girl displayed a touchy ego or an unpleasant disposition, he rejected her. Body proportion and posture represented important physical standards. Can the body wear any type of costume? Will the legs look good when exposed? Does the girl move with "her head up, her spine straight, her stomach and her fanny in"? Those who survived such scrutiny were then asked to dance. Usually, the test included a time step, kicks, backbends, a line of turns, and a ballet combination. Alton's preference was for girls from 18 to 25 years of age, of medium height, with a strong foundation in ballet and tap, a wholesome appearance, and a "flair for wearing clothes."

In *Dance Magazine*, February 1949, Jack Cole published these words of advice for a more professional—and successful audition:

> If the call states that ballet dancers will be auditioned, arrive at the theatre with practice clothes and ballet shoes. Dancers who step forward and apologize for having forgotten their shoes are either suspect of having had little or no school training, since a ballet dancer forgetting shoes is very like dressing for the street and forgetting one's trousers, or of being so scatterbrained and undisciplined as to be of questionable value. Hair dressed up from the neck to show the carriage of the head indicates a dancer who is aware of the basic principles of her craft. Execute the variation as demonstrated or stated exactly; do not improve it or embellish it. Do not ignore the indicated port de bras in an effort to jump through the ceiling, or spin like a top. The director is only interested in ascertaining good training and correct movement habits; the probability of a group of dancers being hired to execute five pirouettes and fall flat on their faces en masse is extremely remote.
>
> A sound technical director does not have bias or prejudice in relation to styles of dance. For him there is only good dancing and bad dancing, whether it be ballet, modern, ethnic, or period. If you are asked to demonstrate a strong, dynamic, primitive figure that pounds into the earth, and you approach it with the delicacy of a *petit battement*, you are a bad dancer. Beautiful *battements*, but bad dancing.
>
> Many times you will be asked to demonstrate a figure in a style that is completely foreign to your training. Try to grasp the basic elements involved quickly, and execute it with good grace and a minimum of pseudo-embarrassment. No editorial comment on the figure or your apparent inability to grasp it is of interest to the director. He is trying to approximate the probable speed at which you learn. Many dancers take ten years to acquire a passable *glissade assemblé*, and ten years are not available before the opening of a show.
>
> Stage managers are not always the most gracious and well-mannered people. Your dance director is usually trying very hard to make you comfortable, not embarrassed or nervous. He does make allowances for a very trying situation. Information requested is usually not important. The director is trying to determine your probable work habits and ability to get along with other people. The neurotic personality may be a brilliant technician but he presents a difficult problem when the schedule gets rough.
>
> If the production is looking for tall blonde girls and you are short and brunette, it is not your fault, nor the dance director's. Preconceived

preferences of type go by the board, if your ability is remarkable. You are more than welcome.

If you have a bad reputation from previous shows—late for rehearsals, irritability, laziness—you may be sure your case history is on file. That is the reason, on many occasions, why good dancers at an audition are not chosen. The director is usually well aware that this audition would be the last sign of effort or talent from the particular person, for the duration of the production.

Don't present letters of introduction. Don't try to talk to the director before the audition. Don't wear costumes, or strange and bizarre practice clothes, and don't bring relatives and friends.

There are never enough well-trained and intelligent dancers. If you are well equipped, you will be eagerly welcomed. Chance plays very little part.

For the *West Side Story* film, Jerome Robbins chose dancers with distinctive personalities as well as technical skill. (*Photo: The Museum of Modern Art Film Still Archives.*)

During the preparation of *West Side Story* in the late 1950s, Jerome Robbins spoke to Victoria Lee of the *New York World-Telegram* about audition preparedness for all the students of acting, dancing, and singing intent on landing a job in show business. A summary of his observations follows. First, a dancer without sufficient training should reconsider auditioning in the first place; technical unpreparedness wastes everybody's time. Second, those whom Jerome Robbins selected had three things in common: They could sing, they could dance, they could act. Third, a vibrant chorus stage personality best complements a strong technique. The modern chorus should not look like a line; each dancer should bring a distinctive personality to the group. Fourth, the best dancers are open to criticism. Fifth, the quick study usually prevails; dancers who can't catch on immediately are of no use to the choreographer. Sixth, dancers without weighty personal problems come through when the going gets rough. Finally, and most important, choreographers prefer dancers who are serious about dancing and their careers.

During the 1970s, Bob Fosse auditioned the best dancers available for *Dancin'*. How did he choose his dancers? The *New York Times* reported this in 1978:

> At the first audition, he tries not to look at the dancers' faces at all. "I want to see their body lines and to see how well they dance. That's usually the first elimination. We go through several of those."
>
> Mr. Fosse said that first he keeps everybody who dances well, "regardless of how they look." Then he looks at their faces, especially their eyes. "I talk to them a little bit, to see what kind of person they are." After that he asks them to sing, still looking for keys to their personality. "They don't give out much when they're trying the dancing steps—they're too nervous. But when they do a song they know, you can generally tell whether there's something inside them by the way they sing it."

With each audition the show dancer must attempt to impress a different choreographer who in turn must satisfy the demands of a different show. There are no magic formulas or shortcuts to success. If they're looking for wholesomeness and you have it, you get a chance. If they're looking for "tits and ass" and you've got 'em, you get a chance. No one makes promises. Nothing is guaranteed. The point of *A Chorus Line* is that the show dancer does it for love. What is done for love, however, might accommodate these suggestions culled from a representative cross-section of potential show dance employers.

ASSETS	LIABILITIES
Poise	If any, don't audition
Timing	
Personality	
Commitment	
Versatility	
Attitude	
Technique	
Training	

The modern show dancer may well be the most overcommitted and undersubscribed performer in the performing arts. To survive, dancers must be tough, intelligent, talented, ambitious, attractive, versatile, well trained, and resilient. Some who were brought up in the chorus graduate to more rewarding careers—like Shirley MacLaine. Unfortunately, most do not. No sympathy, please. Show dancers know that the activity is its own reward.

Movement
Idioms

The movement in show dancing relies on any one or any combination of the following idioms: ballet, jazz dance, tap dance, disco, ethnic dance, folk dance, modern dance, and ballroom. While the prevailing fashion or the beliefs of a dominant choreographer may lead the casual observer to identify one style exclusively with American show dancing, the tradition reaches too far and wide to be subject to the restrictions of or allegiances to any single idiom or style. A dance market that must feed the musical play, musical comedy, burlesque, revue, operetta, opera, television commercials, variety shows, and video can only be serviced properly by the broadest range of movement idioms open to it. Probe your kinetic memory of American musical theater experiences for remembered dance and movement images from *Oklahoma!*, *West Side Story*, *My Fair Lady*, *Gypsy*, *Pippin*, and *A Chorus Line*. Consider each show's intent and how the dance expression in each embraced a specific and exclusive look that in retrospect appears both appropriate and inevitable. If expressive movement represents the "lifeline" of artistic show dancing, then the multi-idiom character represents its personality. American show dance can never be "pure" in the way that we apply the term to ballet or modern dance. However, its polyglot personality—that capacity to speak in several dance languages and continually blend them into a popular mix—seems appropriate to the entertainment of a nation whose population reflects a melting-pot heritage. To extend the analogy further, differences among the dance idioms themselves coincide with differences within each idiom much as differences among people of different races, cultures, and nationalities coincide with differences among people within the same race, culture, and nationality.

Consider the differences among idioms first. Classical ballet utilizes a definite series of steps and movements to create a look that is erect and formal. Modern dance utilizes the entire body along with the air and the

Carol Haney's dances for *Flower Drum Song,* 1958, blended ballet, ethnic, and jazz dance into movement appropriate to the material. (*Photo: Courtesy of Rodgers and Hammerstein.*)

ground in order to project the expressive movement basic to it. Tap dance puts the usually erect and rigid torso to the service of the feet that tap out the sounds, which themselves are the medium and the message of that idiom. Jazz dance makes use of the torso—specifically, isolations of hips, shoulders, and head—in a characteristically rhythmic and ex-plosive way. Some intermediate idioms bridge the gaps between usually separate idioms. George Balanchine's choreography for "Slaughter on Tenth Avenue" from *On Your Toes* could be described as ballet-tap. Fred Astaire's dancing with Ginger Rogers had the look and the sound of ballroom-tap. Dancers in some Broadway shows and television commercials who accompany tap with body isolations employ jazz-tap. Jack Cole's choreography inclined toward ethnic-jazz. And the list goes on. Not surprisingly, theory and execution differences exist within the principal idioms as well as the intermediate forms. Tap dance specialist Maurice Hines makes the distinction between white and black tap dance. For him, the white tap dance taught in most white-owned and -operated dance schools in the United States and epitomized in the show dancing of Tommy Tune is a "high, up in the air" style, characterized by an aristocratic-looking body making polite and brittle tapping sounds. By contrast, the black style consists of close floor work with a relaxed body that "nuzzles" the floor to produce the clear tapping sounds that are the

Fred Astaire's dancing with Ginger Rogers in the film *Top Hat,* 1935, had the look and sound of ballroom-tap. (*Photo: The Museum of Modern Art Film Still Archives.*)

dancers' conversation with the audience. Some call it hoofing, but Hines prefers to call it "laying them down." Since the idea and the method, not the race of the performer, represent the key to each style within an idiom, Hines considers Eleanor Powell and her strong floor work to be an outstanding example of the real black tap style.

In the chronology of idioms, tap or step dancing was the first to surface on the popular American stage. Here was a bold, theatrical, and highly individual way of dancing that both absorbed and adapted nationalistic elements, acrobatics, comedy, virtuosic display, and either classy or flash approaches. Unlike the other major idioms, tap technique calls attention to itself, in any context. It is an act more an end unto itself rather than an expression contributory to other ends. Not surprisingly, tap dominated commercial show dancing during the era of vaudeville, revue, and early musical comedy, when dancing was meant only to entertain in the most direct, obvious, and uncomplicated way. Those elements of tap that survived the maturation of the American musical theater and its accompanying preference for ballet, ballet-jazz, and expressive movement did so primarily in intermediate forms like the ballet-tap, ethnic-tap and the jazz-tap of some recent shows.

Sound provides the key to the appreciation of tap dancing. Whereas ballet, modern dance, and jazz dance employ music as a collaborative component in artistic expression, tap dancing generates the rhythmic sound that in performance either becomes or is embellished by the music itself. The sounds produced emanate from steps in which the entire foot strikes the floor, from taps of the heel or toe, from snapping the fingers or clapping the hands (for rhythm or accent), from slapping the hands on some part of the body, from striking props together or on some hard surface, and, usually, from some combination of the above. The "true" tap dancer addresses the dance to the ear. So much the better if the eyes are pleased as well. Its standards are aural as well as kinetic. At best, tap dancing allows the dancer to draw on a visual component that services an aural message, hopefully in a style distinctive enough henceforth to be associated with that dancer. At worst, tap dancing carries a double liability: You can hear a mistake as well as see it! Therefore, the

Tap dancing dominated the pure entertainment forms of vaudeville, revue, and early musical comedy. (*Photo: Courtesy of Rodgers and Hammerstein.*)

Control of sound, movement, gesture, and expression mark the dancing of Fred Astaire and Ginger Rogers in *Follow the Fleet*, 1936. (*Photo: The Museum of Modern Art Film Still Archives.*)

conscientious tap dancer must focus on rhythm, sound, and silence considerations in music selections, choreography, rehearsal, and performance. Paul Draper defined rhythm in tap dancing as "the pattern of percussive sounds made by the feet within the framework of the accompanying music." This definition implies that the knowledgeable tap dancer works within a sound structure employing the tap sounds as a parallel band of communication that adds to what is already signaled by the rhythm and melody of the music. Meter, beat, rhythm, and melody together form Draper's "musical framework." The term "meter" defines the pattern of regularly repeated strong and weak beats identified by the time signature assigned to the music:

TIME SIGNATURE	BEAT PATTERN
2/4	**B,** b, **B,** b, **B,** b
3/4	**B,** b, b, **B,** b, b
4/4	**B,** b, b, b, **B,** b, b, b

The term "beat" refers to the regularly repeated pulse that determines the rhythmic pattern, like the heartbeat—that contraction and expansion of the heart that sustains the phenomena of life. The term "melody" refers to a succession of musical tones, while the term "rhythm" refers to the outline of the pattern of those tones in time. Tap dancing produces percussive sounds. Their sequence does not constitute melody but rather a conscious musical addition to it. These sounds can match the beat or syncopate; that is, shift the accent. To be effective, the tap dancer must go beyond merely keeping time and strive to add some unique sound contribution within the overall architecture of the dance.

The tap dancing of American show business derived its movement vocabulary from the folk dances of England and Ireland and the American Negro step dances that evolved during the era of minstrel entertainment. In character and history, tap dancing represents a phenomenon that is both popular and American. Popular because the majority of its performers have been more "common" than aristocratic (as in ballet) or intellectual (as in modern dance) and American because its nature—like that of American society itself—represents a fusion of elements from America's immigrant peoples. Its best practitioners aim for control, clarity, and coordination. Control refers to the acquired ability to place the weight-bearing foot in the proper place as if automatically, while simultaneously regulating the precise placement of the tap as well as its most appropriate degree of force. Clarity in tap dancing refers to the precision of sound, movement, gesture, and expression that constitutes articulate tapping. Complete tap dancers must so develop their technique as to be able to execute any required movement and at the same time coordinate the visual element in their performance with the tapping that generates the articulate sounds. Talent, abetted by training and performance, can help the dancer improve timing, pacing, attack, accents, and steps, but without a good back, balance, coordination, and a sense of rhythm, the dancer is likely to fall short of personal expectation and a professional career.

No elements attest more to the breadth and vitality of American tap dancing than the steps whose persistent reinterpretation serve to enrich the idiom. One of the most venerable is the buck-and-wing. *Webster's Third New International Dictionary* defines the buck-and-wing as "a solo tap dance with sharp fast accents, springs, leg flings and heel clicks that was adapted to the stage from a blend of Negro and Irish clog dancing." Essentially, a buck is a stamp of the foot, and a wing is a simple hop with one foot flung out to the side. Being an air step, the wing requires that the arms be extended for balance much like the image of a chicken flapping its wings for balance in movement. Dignified or not, the buck-and-wing forms a core movement from which the routines of the tap dance repertory evolve. That the step reconciles the aural and the visual may account for its influence and importance. Specialty dancers served up three tap wings regularly during the golden days of tap in vaudeville, revue, nightclubs, and early musical comedy. In performance, a dancer would hop on one foot, brush to the side with a toe tap, return to the original position with another toe tap, and land on a third and final sound. Talent and invention brought variety to the execution of wings. The "pump" allowed the winging foot to move up and down in the back, while the "pendulum" the winging foot moved from front to back. Eventually, virtuoso tap dancers developed the five-tap wing—a wing so precisely executed as to brush out a foot with a wing tap and in a split second return it with four more sounds.

Four other steps that proved essential to any tap dancer hoping for a commercial career were "off to Buffalo," "falling off a log," "over the top," and "through the trenches." "Off to Buffalo" and "falling off a log" are travel steps well suited to a routine's need for a flash exit. In the former, one foot continually crosses and recrosses in front of the other in a sideways shuffle motion. In the latter, the dancer employs an alternate crossing of the feet. Tap dancers not yet ready to exit must accent their routines with flash steps, those vigorous and virtuosic steps designed for a single purpose—to make the audience applaud. The classic options: "over the top" and "through the trenches." Leaning forward, the dancer performing the former rises from the floor while alternately swinging each leg from the back across the front of the other leg. The pretense of peril, the projected risk of falling, and the raw energy exerted stimulates the applause. Also leaning forward, the dancer performing the latter engages in backward glides on the outside edge of each foot while the opposite arm reaches into the air. Jerome Robbins used this step in *Gypsy* to mark the transition of Baby June to Dainty June. When needed, the experienced tap dancer might add additional flash with "around the world," a step that requires the support of alternate hands in a crouching position as the legs rotate beneath the body. The flash tap specialists often added breathtaking acrobatic stunts to these steps, like spins, cartwheels, somersaults, back flips, and elevated leaps into a split. As a result, flash tap earned a reputation inclined to be described by adjectives like "vulgar," "loud," "abandoned," and "wild." Other tap dancers, however, relied on more subtle steps. By nature brief and endlessly versatile, the "cramp roll" proved to be an ideal connective in the tap dancer's subtle kinetic vocabulary. The step produces four taps in rapid succession with a toe-heel, toe-heel sound so often a prelude to some more adventurous step in the routine.

The relative immaturity of the show business environment in which tap dancing flourished during the early decades of the twentieth century allowed for the proliferation of standardized tap dance routines—prescribed and detailed sequences of steps regularly followed by members of the chorus as a background to stars and specialty acts. Consider the "bullshit chorus," a famous and widely used combination of tap-dancing clichés designed to be performed by a chorus in the background. Structurally, the routine broke up the standard musical selection of thirty-two bars into four units of eight bars each. Content seldom varied. Eight bars of the time step, eight bars of the cross step, eight bars of buck-and-wing and four bars of "over the top" and "through the trenches." Those dancers in the chorus who were young and inexperienced thought "B.S. Chorus" meant "Boy Scout chorus"; others knew better. In time, it gave way to a more complicated routine known as the "shim sham." This combination divided the thirty-two bars into eight bars each of the "double shuffle," the "crossover," the "tack Annie" (a back-and-forward shuffle), and "falling off a log." These tap dance routines offered a formula that relatively untrained dancers could master, a formula that made no demands of concentration or kinetic awareness on the audience. Those who perpetuated these practices glorified in the mechanics of movement, not in its dramatic or theatrical expression. With vigorous display and high spirits, early tap dancing amused and diverted an audience sensibility that later show dancing would seek to impress and engage.

The stylistic diversity that persists within tap dancing led to a recognition of various approaches to the art and to a variety of names meant to describe each. Some dancers believed in a total emphasis on footwork; they were called hoofers. Some dancers believed in a refined execution of steps combined with elegant body movement and costumes; they were called class acts, or class performers. Some dancers believed in extravagant, acrobatic movements combined with vigorous, strenuous execution; they were called flash acts. A dancer with a predilection for up-tempo music, whirlwind routines, heavy taps, forward-hunched torso, and unhinged arms reflects the so-called old style, epitomized by Eleanor Powell. A dancer drawn to more easy-going routines, delicate taps, lifted rib cage, and classical arm positions engages in the "new style," reflected in the style of dancers who perform relaxed routines with leather soles to a traditional four-to-a-bar tempo in sand-and-dance or soft shoe. All dancers developed characteristic techniques to exploit the potential of their talent and style. Soft-shoe performers favored orchestrations that omit all the notes except the first in a four-to-a-bar measure. Called "stop time," this device permitted the audience to hear and appreciate the language of the dancer's soft, muted steps. Tap dancing is a percussive art. To substitute silence for sound keeps the taps from disintegrating into hopeless cacophony. This "willed silence" can only emphasize the dancer's artistic choices, skill, and control. Dancers drawn less to silence than to a concentration of tap sounds specialized in "riff" techniques that consist of a rapid series of small sounds produced by the heel, the toe, and the heel and toe together. Theirs is a most subtle approach to the art. Cascades of clear, rapidly articulated taps issue from a dancer who hardly appears to move at all. Should anyone assume that these steps, routines, and techniques produce a rigid and exact art, be advised that many tap performers regard tap dancing as an improvisational art and their own routines as subject to extemporaneous modification during performance. Like a jazz musician in a jam session, the tap dancer may plan a beginning, and ending, and a framework, but often there is no rigid formula, no absolute patterns, no invariable set interpretation of some exact sequence. In fact, some of the most famous tap dancers, like Bill "Bojangles" Robinson, built a career on audience expectation of an improvised performance.

The hegemony of tap dancing came to an end during the 1940s. By then, the American musical theater was ready for the great period of artistic and ambitious popular entertainments that *Oklahoma!* would usher in, a revolution in which ballet-oriented movement would be the major dance idiom. Once Rodgers and Hammerstein along with Agnes de Mille introduced the American public to musical love stories and dream ballets, tap dancing proved no longer marketable or even appropriate. Whether you view ballet as a highly stylized mechanism for storytelling (Petipa), a vehicle for structured virtuosity (Balanchine), or an art form built on the refined interaction of music, concept, libretto, choreography, and decor (Diaghilev), there can be no doubt that (in the commercial sense) ballet techniques and style best responded to the design and objectives of the post-1940s serious American musical.

Associations of aristocracy and privilege have always prevailed in the ballet tradition. The kings of France, the czars of Russia, the haut monde of Paris—all favored ballet entertainments. America democratized ballet for its popular theater, and the best musical plays of the great period provided the ideal showcase for its commercial adaptation. Much has been said about *Oklahoma!* as a celebration of American values and a consummate integration of the elements of a musical show; not enough has been said about the show as a beacon for commercial ballet on Broadway. Practical considerations as well as sound artistic ideas account for the overwhelming impact ballet made on show dancing during the 1940s and 1950s. Then, professional American ballet companies were fewer, smaller, less visible, and less aesthetically respectable than the New York and regional companies are today. Shorter seasons, meager salaries, and limited performance exposure forced excellent dancers who were trained in the studios of Edward Caton, Pierre Vladimiroff, and Anatole Oboukhoff to excel in the works of Petipa, Fokine, and Tudor, to shuttle regularly (if they were to support themselves) between their aspirations in ballet companies and jobs in *Oklahoma!, Carousel, Finian's Rainbow, The King and I,* and *Kiss Me Kate.* The superb, versatile, and classically trained dancers who needed a job and loved to dance set new and demanding standards. After them, there was no going back. After them, the new frontier would be ancillary skills, like singing and acting. Ballet training and discipline may account for the desirable carriage, control, and stamina of dancers seeking careers in show business, but it was the evolution of ballet choreography—in which its creators came to absorb and apply elements of folk, modern dance, jazz dance, ethnic dance, and ballroom—that accounts for its usefulness and versatility on the commercial scene.

To some, jazz dance with its primitive, visceral energy may appear to be the philosophical antithesis of ballet and its emphasis on precise steps and disciplined technique. Yet, the show dance that exploits jazz techniques does depend on ballet for such basic movement as pliés, relevés, attitudes, pirouettes, and turns. To ballet technique does jazz show dance look for the lyrical movement needed for contrast with the primitive, percussive quality so natural to its heritage.

The term "jazz dance" cannot be unequivocally defined. Originally, American jazz dance meant tap dance performed to jazz music during the jazz era in American popular culture. Later generations redefined the term to mean an Afro-American vernacular dance with a variety of ethnic elements, performed with a broader use of the entire body and without taps. For others, jazz dance means modern commercial dance, the style used in musical comedy, television, and youth-oriented musical films. If singular movement, not accepted positions or steps, prescribes the nature of jazz dancing, then it is possible that the idiom redefines itself every time it is performed, thus assuming such show dance mutations as ballet-jazz, jazz-tap, rock-jazz, disco-jazz, and street-jazz.

If American jazz dance has been associated with modern show dancing, it is probably because jazz dance embraces the same cultural diversity as American culture itself. To this composite idiom ballet contributes placement and specific movement techniques; East Indian dance adds the angularity, isolations, and upper torso; modern dance adds its grounded, empathetic movement and generous use of space; and tap adds its propensity for rhythm and agile limbs. The artistic freedom that is an American cultural heritage accounts for the continued development of jazz dance as an indigenous form. America grew this spectacular and colorful hybrid in the hothouse of its cultural diversity.

Jazz dancing uses the entire body for kinetic expression. Isolations predominate. Isolations involve a stylized setting apart of specific parts of the body and the moving of each in opposition to the rest. Isolations develop the control and coordination needed, and they constitute a good part of the idiom's technical vocabulary. Head, shoulders, rib cage, and hips submit to individual isolations, as do combinations of head with shoulders, shoulders with rib cage, and so on.

In jazz dancing, all isolations, steps, air work, and turns service rhythm. Stylized walks constitute most traveling steps. Usually, the hips move in the direction of the step: If the step moves forward to the right, the hips push forward to the right; if the step moves forward to the left, the hips push forward to the left. Since other jazz dance styles can embrace opposite characteristics, the mastery of hip isolations becomes prerequisite to the analysis and mastery of this idiom's stage walks. Like isolations, stage walks so respond to rhythm and tempo that speed and the regularity of steps often determine the mood, style, or quality of the walk. The slow walk can convey calm, indolence, fatigue; a fast walk can suggest excitement, intensity, and strength; regularity of step can suggest control, harmony, and organization; and irregularity of step can suggest turmoil, disorder, and confusion. Many of the popular movements associated with stage dancing derive from movement learned in isolations. Hip isolations produce the bump, head and neck isolations produce a head roll, rib cage or upper torso isolations facilitate the layout—wherein the upper torso arcs backward from the waist—and shoulder isolations make possible many variations of the shoulder shake or shimmy.

Although the term "jazz dance" has come to mean show dancing for many in the dance world, particularly those with show business aspirations, many of its traditions and much of its choreography differ substantially from the Broadway dancing that adapts jazz dance to the stage, film, and video vehicles. If anything, show dance today is nothing more than some talented choreographer's conception of what some superbly trained young dancers should execute for the show or to the music. It

For *West Side Story,* Jerome Robbins turned to a jazz dance idiom that used the entire body for kinetic expression. (*Photo: The Museum of Modern Art Film Still Archives.*)

has always been more of a style or a trend than a hybrid form with a variable mix of constituent elements. At times, its choreography, routines, and the look of its dancers reflect the period style demanded by the material; otherwise the style takes on the strongly personal character of the choreographer. Put in historical perspective, the dance styles that have endured in twentieth-century American show dance can be divided very roughly into decades. Within each period, the performance style can be straight—that is, an attempt at exact duplication of the period—or camp—an attempt to comment on the period, usually for laughs. To set a show in exact period style, choreographers must understand and appreciate the total dance look of the period and exercise skill and discipline in communicating that look to an audience. Most successful choreographers research extensively in the pursuit of authentic style when they are choreographing something that is meant to have a period flavor. Books of and on the period that reveal behavior, mores, and social etiquette can be useful. Pictures and films that capture the poses, steps, and movement of the time provide clues if not the key to setting the show. As a choreographer confided during a recent revival, "We transport ourselves in the way we move, talk, look at each other, sit down—everything!"

Since 1975, Lee Theodore and her American Dance Machine have been reconstructing, documenting, performing, and thus preserving representative dance numbers from each of the major periods that together make up the American show dance tradition. Hers is a philosophical as well as a practical mission. For too long, the dances of the American musical stage have been allowed to die with the closing of the original production. Valuable treasures from the repertories of Jack Cole, Jerome Robbins, Agnes de Mille, Michael Kidd, Bob Fosse, and others could be lost forever unless an organization were created to renew their dance life in performance and so ensure more continuity to the stage dancing tradition. On a practical level, the concept behind the American Dance Machine can serve to channel to choreographers appropriate royalties for their professional contributions. In the past, show dance choreographers suffered from an accepted professional system that brought handsome royalties to the creators of script and score and comparatively little financial reward to the creators of a show's dances, whose work could be replicated without any additional payment being made to them. In future, people interested in duplicating choreography will have to pay royalties as well, and this will eliminate much of the plagiarism that has victimized theater dance creators for decades.

Whatever the dance idiom employed or the style of dancing preferred, criteria must be established that measure effectiveness and guide choreographers in creative exploration. Whether in period or personal style, the dancing of a show should be appropriate to the material. Whatever the talent, inspiration, and working methods employed, the results should be innovative and distinctive. If a dancer is expected to give generously of self to become a complete professional, so must the maker of dances contribute generously of self to make dances unlike any others. Though the goal may be clear, the successful realization of a show dance takes talent, time, commitment, and taste.

Undoubtedly, the balance of priorities given to major show dance idioms will shift as successful new choreographers enter the field. What matters most for the dancing is that the aspiring young professional who chooses this life be skilled in all idioms and most styles. If so, the future will be bright—if unpredictable.

Education
and
Training

Dancers hoping for careers in show business must be better trained and more broadly versatile than ever before. The environment they choose to inhabit has become kinetically sensitive, and if actors and singers now train in movement, then dancers must specialize in it. Proper training takes time; at least ten years might be needed to produce a dancer with a well-rounded background. To young performers raised in a climate of instant gratification and too frequently dazzled by the occasional example of overnight success, the prospect of ten years of serious, diligent training might appear prohibitive. Consequently, two dangers surface. The dancer might be tempted to rush or cut corners in order to accommodate ambition. The dancer might be tempted to learn routines rather than learn how to dance. Unfortunately, every section of the country supports at least one studio or teacher eager to peddle mendacious dreams and their attendant routines. Instead, the serious dancer must pursue technique, that mastery of the physical tools of expressive movement by which dancers achieve their effects. Technique ensures the ability to execute at will all the steps in an acknowledged repertory. Technique affords access to performance virtuosity accomplished with consummate ease. Technique makes the aesthetic experience possible by allowing the audience to focus on the dance and not on the obvious energy and discipline expended in shaping the steps and the movements. Fred Astaire's television dance partner Barrie Chase advised, "Without a responsive body you can't do what you want to do. Technique frees me to—dance."

In the past, show dancers took their training where they found it. Consider this reminiscence from tap dancer Pete Nugent: "I won a contest when I was about eleven. I couldn't tell you what kind of dance it was, but it wasn't good. I learned it in the street. That's where we all learned." Others like tap dancer Honi Coles got their training on the job. Speaking of the environment of Harlem's Lafayette Theatre in the 1930s, he lamented to Kevin Grubb, *Dance Magazine*, September 1983:

> At the Lafayette, you didn't just do your specialty act, you did everything: sing, dance, act—the works. That's one of the things that's missing in the business today. There's no place to *really* learn your craft. You go to an audition, get a part dancing, and that's as far as it goes. But at the Lafayette, I got a real education.

As American dance, its public, and its choreography matured, self-trained dancers found little work. Today's level of show dancing demands technique, and technique requires formal dance training. In the comparatively short period between *On Your Toes* and *Oklahoma!*, George Balanchine and Agnes de Mille managed to sweep away the street and social dance basis for a career in stage dance and substitute instead the manner, discipline, and language of ballet. Suddenly, ballet technique replaced tap talent, ballroom glamour, and acrobatic oddity in the affections of producers, choreographers, and dancers. Ray Bolger, the successful eccentric dancer and male soloist in Balanchine's "Slaughter on Tenth Avenue" from *On Your Toes*, was one of the earliest dance stars to recognize the importance of technique to even the commercial dancer. "The more you study technique," he said, "the more you add to your dancing. In order to satirize a ballet or any other step, you should be able first to do any step properly. Many comic dancers don't progress because they don't study deeply."

The overwhelming consensus of opinion drawn from teachers, choreographers, and dancers supports the proposition that ballet technique provides indispensable training for any dancer interested in a show business career. Ballet is a foundation technique. It offers the student discipline, a movement vocabulary, standards that favor precision and clarity of movement, and a style that gives the impression of being both ethereal and strong. Proper ballet training produces impressively postured bodies supported by a strong vertical spine, stretched muscles, fluid motion, and graceful arms assimilated into an altogether aristocratic bearing. It offers the ideal system for gaining control of the dancer's instrument—the body.

Since ballet combines effectively with other dance idioms, even the

Ballet training offers the dancer a movement vocabulary, plus standards that favor precision and clarity of movement. *Flashdance,* 1983. (*Photo: The Museum of Modern Art Film Still Archives.*)

most outspoken jazz dance professionals acknowledge the role ballet training plays in a dancer's personal development and professional career. In *Dance Magazine*, May 1978, jazz teacher Ron Daniels advised that "a beginning student should be aware that jazz dance is to ballet as jazz music is to classical music. Jazz dance improvises on basic, defined ballet movements." The Bob Fosse dancer Ann Reinking trains in ballet. As she puts it in *Dance Magazine*, February 1978:

> It's probably not true for everybody, of course, but *for me,* for me, I find jazz doesn't have enough construction to it, in order to make me advance myself as a dancer. You don't get enough strength, you don't get enough discipline, you don't get enough real warm-up. So I go ballet, just because it's healthier for me. I find that if I get stronger in my ballet technique, then my jazz technique improves, too.

Even Gus Giordano when speaking of his jazz dance company admitted in *Dance Magazine*, February 1981, "All of my company members take daily ballet classes at my Dance Center, so their concert work takes on the flavor of—like wings! The alphabet of these dancers is ballet, but their greatest thrust is in jazz." The Tony Award–winning dancer Hinton Battle (*Sophisticated Ladies*) studied ballet on a scholarship at the School of American Ballet and accepted work in musical theater early in his career only to support a strong interest in ballet. When George Balanchine decided that Battle was too short for the New York City Ballet, Battle moved on to critical success as a Broadway dancer performing in a variety of styles in shows like *Dancin', Sophisticated Ladies,* and *The Tap Dance Kid.* Although these recent career opportunities have led him to "speaking with his feet" in tap dancing, Battle acknowledges the continuing impact of ballet. In *Dance Magazine,* November 1981, he wrote, "Ballet discipline is very strong and makes you keep your standards very high. On Broadway, you can sort of slack off a little and skip classes, but, after a while, it shows." Once equipped with ballet technique, most stage dancers set out to acquire new kinds of movement for a body already prepared to absorb them. Jazz dance and tap skills add an attractive adjunct to a performer's professional skills.

Jazz dance training exposes the dancer to the prevalent mode of today's show dance. To achieve that bold, sexy, and exuberant look, jazz dance students exercise the pelvis, rib cage, head, neck, shoulders, chest, arms, and hips in pursuit of that hallmark of the form—a pliant, flexible and undulating torso. To the ballet training that produces a physical carriage and look that can be aloof and virginal, jazz dance adds the unbridled energy and looseness of movement that can be worldly and visceral. What makes jazz dance so popular and appropriate to our time is its total body response to musical rhythm; and rhythm, more than melody or harmony, dominates the popular, youth-oriented music of our time. Watch her body in *Flashdance,* his body in *Footloose,* any video by Michael Peters (cochoreographer of *Dreamgirls* and choreographer of Michael Jackson's videos), or some television commercials, and what you will see are the visual manifestations of the basic rhythmic pulse of the musical accompaniment.

In jazz dance training and choreography, personality accounts for stylistic variations within the form. Study with Luigi and you get a lot of ballet-jazz. Work with Matt Mattox and you focus on a fast footwork style of jazz. Dance in a Fosse show and the rhythm response will most likely be choreographed right down to the isolation of the left eyebrow. Since the matter of jazz dance represents a melting pot of many dance idioms, teachers and choreographers are free to devise dance material from their own background, physique, ideas, emotional makeup, and aesthetic principles. Without the universally recognized codification of steps so typical of ballet, jazz dance instruction and choreography revolves more around personal communication. The idiom encourages strong personal and professional bonds to be formed between instructors and protégés, choreographers and dancers. Think of Jack Cole and Gwen Verdon, Gwen Verdon and Bob Fosse, Bob Fosse and Ann Reinking.

All jazz training begins with warm-ups. Pliés in parallel, turned-out, and turned-in positions warm up the legs and knees. Side bends and contractions warm up the area of the abdomen and lower back. Floor exercises warm up the muscles of the hips and waist. Usually, isolations follow the warm-up. Here, instruction concentrates on specific movement for parts of the body like the shoulders, rib cage, and hips performed independently of other interconnected parts. For example, isolations could involve a lifting and lowering of the shoulders while holding the head and torso as still as possible. Variations could include a shoulder roll, a continuous movement of the shoulders from up to back to down to front, or a shimmy, the rapid and continuous movement of one shoulder forward as the other thrusts back. The hip isolations so visible in disco dancing can be achieved by raising, then lowering, the hips from side to side, tilted forward to backward or set in the continuous circular motion of a grind. Like the hips, the rib cage can be isolated for movement from side to side, front to back, as well as in circular fashion. Effective rib cage isolations depend on keeping the shoulders and hips as still as possible. Afterward, a class might move on to learning a combination, a sequence of structured steps with a beginning, middle, and end—a fragment of what when joined with other combinations might result in a complete dance. To learn a combination properly, the student should focus on the rhythm of the music, the tempo, the structure of the movement and its direction, and the footwork, steps, and style. Inevitably, the best students will bring much of their individual movement characteristics to the combination and make it their own within acceptable limits.

The revival, during the past fifteen years, of tap dancing in the American musical has made training in the idiom a desirable addition to the show dancer's repertory. Fast footwork and the expression of rhythm in tap sounds characterize the form. Standard tap instruction prescribes that movement be executed from an erect standing position with knees bent and arms held comfortably at the sides. A relaxed lower body is essential; undue tension in the legs, ankles, and feet inhibits control, the shifts in body weight, and the development of the clear and rapid sounds expected from the technically strong dancer. Basic instruction involves learning the steps, hops, brushes, slaps, shuffles, and cramp rolls, pullbacks, and wings that produce the taps of tap dancing. In a step, the ball of the foot makes contact with the floor as the dancer shifts weight to that foot. Properly executed, steps produce clean, sharp sounds of approximately the same volume. Eventually, the dancer learns to control the sound level of the steps regardless of body position, speed, or direction. The hop consists of a straight up-and-down movement off the floor of about a quarter inch or more. Properly executed, the hop lands on the ball of the foot with the heel in the air. The dancer's foot produces a brush by briefly striking the ball of the foot on the floor as the foot moves forward, backward, to the side, or on the diagonal. The slap combines the initial motion of a brush with a step usually forward, back, or to the side. For many dancers, the most basic of basic steps is the shuffle, a small movement comprising a forward brush and a backward brush. While the thigh moves the leg forward, sideways, or back, the ankle controls the brief contact with the floor. The cramp roll combines steps and heel drops into four sound patterns such as step, heel, step, heel or step, step, heel, heel. The standard: evenly placed sounds. Popular function: to facilitate landings from a variety of jumps. When the ball of the foot strikes the floor while a dancer's body pulls backward in the air, the tap step is known as a pullback. Eventually, the tap dance student will be introduced to wings, the most famous of the basic tap steps for the American stage. To execute a wing, fling the foot to the side and as it returns for a landing, strike the floor before achieving the original position. The simplest wing creates three sounds: the scrape of the initial movement and the two sounds of the slap on the return movement.

To the aspiring show dancer adept in the techniques of ballet, jazz, and tap, the American Dance Machine offers instruction in the period style needed for performing well in the revivals of American musicals that constitute the majority of scholastic, collegiate, dinner theater, summer theater, and Broadway performances. In addition to its stated goals of preserving American theater dance in the performance repertory of its companies, the American Dance Machine aims to serve as a research center, an instrument of video documentation, a living archive, and an impetus to the scholarly documentation of specific show dances so that qualified dancers intent on a show business career may receive the most comprehensive and professionally oriented training available.

Individual courses reflect the movement and style characteristics of show dancing of the 1920s, 1930s, 1940s, 1950s, and 1960s. Students learn by observation and imitation. By looking back in order to preserve the best, the American Dance Machine may become a vital force in America's show dance future.

Be advised: The current level of widespread and excellent training opportunities does not guarantee entry, much less success, in so competitive a profession. Anatomy, talent, early training, and innate musicality figure prominently in building a show dance career. Most bodies dance, fewer dance well, and only a few dance well and look great in the process. For most of us, the body represents the structure and substance of self. For the dancer, the body is all of that as well as professional destiny. Size, shape, weight, alignment of head, neck, shoulders, back, hips, legs and feet, muscle strength, control, and coordination—all figure into the inventory of a show dancer's professional potential. Early training augments the prospect of the basic equipment. The critical training years for girls range from eight to fifteen; the critical years for boys range from eleven to eighteen years. After that, dance instruction can affect the most desirable use of a dancer's physique but will not, cannot, alter the prospects of the physique itself. A dancer's career is a short one. Physical resources decline when growth stops, and the average body stops developing around the age of twenty-one. Consequently, most dancers peak between ages twenty-five and thirty-five. However, star dancers can be marketable long after.

Since music presides over the marriage of the body to movement, a sensitivity to music complemented by some knowledge of its rudiments gives the dancer so endowed an extraordinary advantage. Too often, dancers become so involved with the technique of manipulating torso and limbs that they neglect altogether the sound that accompanies the dance. To help their bodies respond to the music, dancers should study those elements shared by music and dance—namely, rhythm, form, and dynamics. Desirable, too, might be an awareness of melody, harmony, syncopation, and counterpoint. Musical studies for the dancer need not be dry, dull, or excessively theoretical. The dancer's body can be made an effective agent of musical discovery. The heartbeat teaches rhythm. Gestures embody dynamics. Vocalized song instructs in principles of composition and form. Should a dancer choose to pursue a college degree, general education options in Music Appreciation, General Music Methods, or Music Fundamentals could introduce the future professional to the nature of an art that both generates and accompanies dance. The collegiate experience offers the stage dancer additional incentives. A dancer is a person as well as a body. No artist can aspire to personal and professional aims of consequence without intellectual achievement and self-awareness. The college experience can be a positive one for the show dancer, although it is definitely not the best option for all. Intensive academic training could prove counterproductive to the kinetically gifted but educationally backward or inarticulate dancer. In addition, some collegiate dance programs promise broad and intensive training but deliver only pleasant diversion—a deceit that could seriously compromise a young person's commitment to an activity and a career. When Broadway dancer Wayne Cilento was asked if dancers with commercial potential should be directed to college or Broadway, he responded in *Dance Magazine*, March 1984:

> I chose college, but I was eighteen and had never danced before. It's ultimately an individual's decision. In college, you go through intensive training with minimal distractions and a lot of theory. If you've had a lot of dance training in your early years, you may be ready to tackle Broadway. For me, college was an essential, but it is *not* the real world.

At that same panel discussion, Broadway dancer Niki Harris said, "I am convinced that you *can* have it all." In addition to dancing and teaching dance, Niki earned a bachelor's as well as a master's degree.

Obviously, no one path leads directly to a show dancing career. In addition to training and instruction, all aspirants should examine the nature of their ambition, their economic and social priorities, and the level of commitment to the world they hope to enter. Though the rewards are sweet, the competition is keen.

11

Choreography

Choreographer: A maker of the figures and steps in dancing. Stage or film choreographer: A creator-interpreter who collaborates with others within a dictatorship. Director-choreographer: The dictator who assumes all creative and interpretative responsibility for the project. The rise of the American musical in artistry and construction during this century paralleled similar positive developments in its dancers, dancing, the makers of the dances, and the importance of their contribution. The dance director of early musical comedy and revue regarded dancing as a means to applause—nothing more. Formula dances reigned. Imagination meant a new approach to the formula. The choreographic principles adhered to became the musical staging clichés of the century. Custom demanded strict adherence to tempo, beat, or musical phrasing. Custom demanded that tempo be accelerated near the end of a number to drive home the big finish. Custom demanded that the dance idea evolve from the lyric. For the dance director "research" meant "study the lyric" so that during rehearsal, a plausible routine could be built around it. Custom demanded that the standard staging formula go something like this: Principal sings the song and exits while the chorus enters dancing to the music of the same song; then, the principal might return to join the chorus or for a solo reprise, in which case the chorus would exit and return only for the finale. Producers valued dances with immediate impact on the public. The prospect of commercial spin-offs into the ballroom or social dancing arenas appealed to the profit-minded show business employer. First introduced onstage, the Charleston swept the nation, setting American boys and girls to flinging their feet to its tricky steps with the pep and energy the dance demands. Of course, the dance demands that the sheet music be bought so that the musicians can play it. When Bobby Connolly devised the sensational "Varsity Drag" for *Good News,* he did so not only for the show but to promote the dance with the

173

public. What more likely platform than the stage to launch the exuberant, Charleston-style dance as the latest national craze? A contemporary press release revealed this dual commitment: "In the musical comedies upon which I am now at work, I am attempting to launch several dances which I feel will claim a goodly share of the public imagination, excess energy and time. The musical comedy stage aims to teach as well as please."

Within this unapologetically commercial milieu there emerged a few dance directors of talent and imagination whose innovations constitute a legacy of techniques and practices as valid today as they were fifty years ago. Busby Berkeley devised numbers wherein different sections of the chorus danced to different rhythms, thus permitting the shifting accents to break up the uniformity of the sounded accents associated with the precision chorus. LeRoy Prinz "broke the line" too; he allowed different sections of the chorus to execute different types of movement simultaneously. By making full use of the stage, tap dancer Pete Nugent challenged the custom of the stationary chorus in a "B.S." routine. Then, chorus choreography favored standard steps and predictable posturing executed in a straight line. Today, choreography moves its figures around the entire stage in any number of geometric, organic, or idiosyncratic patterns in order to structure expressive movement thoughtfully coordinated with the objectives of the show. To be sure, show dance choreography profited from the comparatively recent cross-fertilization of choreographers and dancers from ballet companies, modern dance troupes, and a variety of film media. When actors accept roles that seem beyond their reach technically, physically, or emotionally, they attribute the activity to a sound artistic need to stretch their capabilities while allowing audiences to experience with them this added dimension and daring. Why shouldn't the same be true for dancers? Think of Diana Adams dancing for de Mille in *Oklahoma!*, then for George Balanchine in *Agon*. Think of Janet Eilber working in the Martha Graham Company as well as appearing on Broadway with the American Dance Machine. For many performers and choreographers, show dance represents a career option.

What is a show dance choreographer? What are the requirements for the position? What are the standards for this work? Today's musical show choreographer must be a successful collaborator equally adept at working with the cocreators of the production and the dancers who people it. The modern musical that employs dancers does so not merely to enhance the songs with dances but to build the show itself on the considerable expressive resources of purposeful movement. Should the trend toward skeletal, nonbook shows persist, then only master director-choreographers need apply. To them comes accountability for a show's content as well as its musical staging and dances.

Since choreography must be worked out on dancers' bodies, the successful choreographer recognizes the cooperative nature of his relationship with them as collaborators. A choreographic idea cannot be expressed in a dance independent of the specific body, technical skills, individuality, and movement characteristics of the dancer chosen for the occasion. The merits of choreography and musical staging have always been credited solely to the creator; only now are the dancers getting credit for their contributions. Standard practice in midcentury show business even allowed choreographers to assume credit for material originated by the dancers themselves. According to Honi Coles, the team of Coles and Atkins was invited to join the cast of *Gentlemen Prefer Blondes* in 1949. When rehearsals under choreographer Agnes de Mille proved unproductive, the composer Jule Styne suggested that the dancers work out a routine themselves and then get de Mille to look at it. Coles and Atkins engaged an arranger who specialized in tap dance routines so that together they could come up with a Broadway caliber routine. De Mille liked the material and told them to keep it in the show. Credited or not, the process betrays the substance and spirit of genuine collaboration. Fortunately, recent practices disallow the questionable ethics of such earlier procedures. Today, the dramatic premise of *A Chorus Line* underscores the need that show choreographers recognize the contributions of dance artists who willingly and lovingly commit totally to the show dance experience. Even the most thorough, prepared, and cerebral choreographers armed with preconceived dance material cannot avoid the formidable resources available in the inventive capacities and movement nuances of their dancers. When Michael Bennett confides that, when choreographing the part of Cassie, he profited from the availability of Donna McKechnie, the statement implies more than just the obvious tribute to a favorite dancer. The statement acknowledges the choreographer's intended alertness for the individual variants in movement and gesture, the particularized deviations in execution, or the individual quirks in personality or temperament inherent in a dancer's presence that can, should, and *do* enrich—even shape—the eventual dance.

A suitable creative atmosphere aids and abets the collaborative process. When Tommy Tune and Thommie Walsh took over *My One and Only,* revamped the entire production, and salvaged what might have become a major disaster, they attributed the positive changes to the creative environment made possible by the takeover. Tune acknowledges the importance of maintaining a creative climate during the evolution of a musical show. For him, a creative environment spawns "higher work." When the "climate is right . . . young things . . . grow." It is no secret that in a Tommy Tune show, the creative climate begins and is sustained by Tommy Tune.

Although choreographic creativity cannot be taught, the skills needed to complement given talent can be learned. Method comes from experience, as do steps, styles, confidence, and taste. Seldom do major stage dance careers follow identical paths of study, apprenticeship, and self-discovery. Whether the path leads from ballet, academia, the chorus, or nightclubs, most successful show choreography careers emerge when, at that critical juncture, the chosen tackle their job armed with all the skills of the trade. Even a modest, regional career in staging dances demands mastery of a wide range of dance techniques. Should the choreographer be unable or unwilling to demonstrate ideas to the dancers, the use of another choreographer or choreographic assistant is advised. It is possible to devise movements for others without the technical proficiency to perform them oneself. Choreographers deal in vision; dancers deal in execution. One envisions movement, the others embody it. Armed with training, experience, and skill, the stage choreographer must be able to look back as well as forward. All creative work emerges from a sound tradition. Even the artistic decision to reject the past acknowledges acquaintance with that which is to be rejected. Since the language of movement can be universal and timeless, master choreographers absorb the past rather than reject it. All agreed that Bob Fosse's staging of *Pippin* served its material, but it also treated the audience to a kaleidoscope of dance images from minstrelsy, vaudeville, film, jazz, and burlesque. Fosse understands that to look back and rediscover tradition need not mean a rigid adherence to rules and regulations. The beacon of support that tradition provides allows the choreographer to find his own way.

Although instruction and training alone do not make a choreographer, it is possible to suggest some elementary standards for aspirants to follow. First: Successful stage choreography aims for movement as metaphor for the dramatic or theatrical message of the show. Vacuous and predictable routines serve as period commentary only. Second: Inventive staging counts, particularly if it in no way violates the integrity of a show's substance. The staging must fit. It must work within and for its particular context. No sympathy whatsoever must extend to

Carol Haney's concern for fluid movement characterizes this moment from *Flower Drum Song,* 1958. (*Photo: Courtesy of Rodgers and Hammerstein.*)

last season's answer to this season's problem. Borrowing can destroy the prospects of a business in which success breeds imitation. Third: Effective dances flow. The steps, kicks, jumps, traveling steps, and turns must move as freely and naturally as if the dance always was and just happened to be discovered intact during one miraculous rehearsal. Dancers tell us that great movement enjoys its own logic and that the dances of great choreographers flow from step to step inevitably. Nothing inhibits the success of artworks in time more than static development or labored progression. Fourth: Show choreography profits from motivated movement. Combinations without cause work against the best interests of the product. Fifth: Show dance courts contrast. Excessive uniformity promotes boredom. Why pay today's prices to endure monotony? Sixth: Choreography and dancing make clarity of communication a priority. Purposeful dancing fails if the public must guess at what the moment was meant to be.

Sound methods support the pursuit of fundamental standards. At the outset of any choreographic enterprise looms the question: How to begin? Choreography begins with the choreographer alone or the choreographer with dancers. Choose the former and be prepared to research and rely exclusively on your own means. You might begin by dancing in character to music. Let the body register a kinetic response to the choreographic task. A gesture may register as exactly right, then a step, and later, a combination. It is important to concentrate and measure the body's response fairly and accurately. Discourage flailing about in search of inspiration or the "lucky accident." When properly applied, the method can produce impressive results. Some choreographers must work from within themselves before they can relay their decisions to the dancers.

Should you prefer to work with the dancers, you might begin with improvisations. Create in the studio an atmosphere, situation, or mood approximate to the desired product. Encourage the dancers to free themselves, to be totally absorbed by the manufactured environment. In both the London and New York productions of *Cats,* choreographer Gillian Lynne began with cat improvisations: cats scratching, stretching, pawing, leaping, and stalking. External stimuli were introduced to help the dancers "stamp the style of cats on everything they did." The studio bulletin board overflowed with pictures of cats, cat food advertisements, and "cat" words like "catalogue," "cats for sale," and the like. Improvisations prove particularly helpful in musical staging when the choreographer must work with actors. When Graciella Danielle began to work on the New York Shakespeare Festival's *Pirates of Penzance,* she delighted in what the actors brought physically to rehearsals in their pursuit of characterization. As a result, Danielle choreographed by shaping the actors' own movement as opposed to imposing her movement decisions on them.

Once begun, the choreographic process must address the critical area of motivation. All choreography values motivated movement. Theater choreography in a dramatic context values it even more. The principle applies to all idioms of show dancing. Paul Draper offered this advice to the student of tap dancing: "Nothing in dancing is so shatteringly empty as three choruses filled with sound and fury and arms and legs and no remote suggestion as to why. Nothing is so meaningless as a series of steps without communicable motivation. It makes no difference how difficult the steps nor how expertly performed." In *The Art of Making Dances,* Doris Humphrey proclaimed that "movement without a motivation is unthinkable. Some force is a cause for change of position, whether it is understandable or not." The matter of motivation becomes even more critical in stage dancing because the movers usually represent characters in a dramatic context or symbolize the context itself, dancing at that moment in order to contribute to the evening's plot, concept, or design. Choreographer Graciella Danielle on motivation in theater dance in *Dance Magazine,* January 1984: "One of the problems I see with today's choreography in theater is motivation. Why are these people dancing? I mean, you can't stage a five-minute ballet in the middle of a show simply because it looks good. There's got to be a reason." Although drama directors and choreographers use different approaches to and methods of securing motivated movement, both agree that it must be understood by the performers and registered in their behavior. For the stage dance choreographer, the quest begins with a vigorous analysis or an intuitive assimilation of script and score. How might the dancing become an extension of the show's material or intent? How might composition, steps, and tone serve all artistic decisions? Once determined, lines of communication must be kept open between choreographers and their dancers. Counseling dancers on the "why" must accompany if not preface any demonstration of the "how." Both responsibilities come with the territory.

In theater dance, concern for dance integration accompanies the concern for motivation. Like song, dance respresents an artificial convention audiences must accept if the show is to be as believable as it is artistically coherent. Rodgers and Hammerstein understood the value of songs that extended the plot in a way that achieved a seamless whole—the so-called integrated musical. Indeed, their working methods gave top priority to discussion, argument, and then total agreement on the placement of the songs. Today's critics and audiences expect a show's dances to be integrated as well. Probably, the best possible method for ensuring dramatically and theatrically logical dance integration is to include the choreographer in the creative process. In the most impressive and seamless movement musicals like *West Side Story* and *A Chorus Line,* the director-choreographer originated the concept and commandeered the creative process. That the dance director was brought in after the completion of the book and score accounted for much of the "dance as wallpaper" routines of past musical shows. If for no other reason, *West Side Story* would deserve everlasting benediction from the show-dance community because Jerome Robbins was the first to conceive a show for expressive movement and engineer the contributions of author, composer, and lyricist in order to ensure the inviolability of his vision. Properly achieved, the integrated dance musical flows from words to song to movement without a discernible break. The action of the show never stops, because the action of the show *is* the show.

The search for fresh, new choreographic ideas joins motivation and

Jerome Robbins integrated words, song, and dance in the ballet "The Small House of Uncle Thomas" from the film version of *The King and I. (Photo: The Museum of Modern Art Film Still Archives.)*

integration in the first rank of a show choreographer's concerns. What to do? How to proceed? No sure answer. Many successful stagings result from nothing more than trial and error. The smash hit on opening night impresses with a perfection and inevitability that may not have existed in rehearsal, previews, or out of town. The secret that produced such excellence exists only in hindsight. So, what's wrong with trial and error? Hal Prince used it; Jerome Robbins used it; so did Bob Fosse. The point is eventually to get it right and not be too concerned by the number of alternatives rejected on the way to the best possible staging and choreography.

In order to get it right, the novice might review such basic elements of dance as form, pattern, dynamics, style, and virtuosity.

Form in dance represents the shape of the whole; that is, the structure of the dance in time. Like the lyric that exists in time, dance form submits to organizational principles like beginning, middle, and end or theme, variation, and restatement. For instance, a dance in the service of *West Side Story* might begin with a meeting: Tony and Maria enter from opposite sides of the stage and meet during the dance at the gym. Their attraction may develop during a middle section where they dance together and end when dramatic situation forces them to retreat to opposite sides of the stage.

Within form, dance communicates through a systematic arrangement of position and step elements known as *pattern*. Lyrics reflect pattern in rhythm and rhyme. Music reflects pattern in the rhythm of song beats. Dance reflects pattern in planned combinations of flowing or accented steps in symmetry or asymmetry. Three ingredients constitute pattern: the step, the combination, the arrangement. A step involves the action of body movement that is brought to rest again. A combination involves joining together a series of steps. Arrangement involves an organization

A circular dance pattern on display in the ballet from *An American In Paris*, 1951. (*Photo: The Museum of Modern Art Film Still Archives.*)

of dancers performing the combinations. A symmetrical arrangement creates a restful and aesthetically pleasing image through the similar arrangement of dancers on both sides of a real or imaginary line. To make Maria and Tony enter from opposite sides of the stage and meet facing each other on both sides of the imaginary line that divides the stage in half is to suggest a pleasing and peaceful moment during what will soon become an arena of explosive conflict. Asymmetrical patterns stimulate restless, exciting images through an unbalanced arrangement of dancers. Generally, formal and decorous dances favor symmetry; spontaneous and violent dances favor asymmetry.

Those who dance the patterns within the form submit to principles of *dynamics* that control the relative forces exerted by bodies in motion. The dynamics of music regulate the degrees of volume in performance; the dynamics of dance regulate the degrees of kinesthetic strength and weakness regulated by the choreography. Dynamic variations bring to dance the contrasts most apparent to an audience: moments of energy,

The unique expressive quality Fred Astaire and Ginger Rogers brought to their partnership gave their dancing a singular and inimitable style. *Flying Down to Rio,* 1933. (*Photo: The Museum of Modern Art Film Still Archives.*)

Dynamic variations control the force exerted by the bodies of dancers, as in this athletic sequence from the film version of *Carousel*. (*Photo: Courtesy of Rodgers and Hammerstein.*)

vigor, and power contrasted with moments of weakness, frailty, and calm.

Style makes a statement independent of dynamics. Style is the specific manner of expression peculiar to a work, a period, or a personality. It implies the purposeful and consistent choice of expressive ingredients to achieve a characteristic manner. In the musical theater, dance styles most often reflect the period of the show, the methods of the choreographer, or the tone of the material, whichever value rises most in the pecking order of collaborative priorities. Some choreographers adapt their talent to the material; others adapt the material to the talent. Jerome Robbins took the former course in *Fiddler on the Roof*; Bob Fosse took the latter in *Pippin* and *Chicago*.

Only after settling on form, pattern, dynamics, and style do serious choreographers turn to performance *virtuosity* to generate audience excitement. While dance in the mature musical theater exists to serve the book, dance steps and combinations can and do draw attention to themselves, particularly when an exceptionally talented dancer defies the laws of balance and gravity to meet the demands of the choreography.

In the presentational world of the American musical, controlled virtuosity works like an effective song—both stimulate applause.

In order to get it right, the novice might examine the ways in which dance can function in a dramatic or theatrical context. Once the creative-interpretative collaboration determines the amount and place of dance in the concept of the show, the choreographer is free to experiment with its use in any number of ways—to carry the plot, establish atmosphere, embody a theme, replace dialogue, generate comedy, extend a dramatic moment, or produce a frankly overwhelming spectacle. Of course, these functions overlap.

Where the nonlyric theater employs dialogue and action to carry the plot to another logical stage of development, the musical theater relies on song or movement. The "Dream Ballet" that concludes Act I of *Oklahoma!* takes the plot from Laurie's indecision to an action whose motive the ballet reveals only to the audience. When a show needs a rapid forward movement of the plot, dance can initiate, advance, or complete the desired dramatic action. In *West Side Story,* Jerome Robbins used dance to initiate conflict between the Jets and the Sharks in the "Prologue," advance the conflict during "The Dance at the Gym," and complete the action during "The Rumble." If needed, dance can telescope the action of the plot; that is, carry it some distance in a disproportionate amount of time. Through a dance sequence of only forty measures of music, Tony and Maria see each other during "The Dance at the Gym," approach, and fall in love—an action that could have taken pages of dialogue to develop.

Mood submits readily to dance expression because the human body registers in muscular tension and movement the visible impact of thought and emotion on a character. Since strong emotions like joy or sadness register quickly in facial expression, posture, or gesture, their re-creation in dance art is likely to transmit clear signals to an audience eager to participate in the theatrical event. Although music reinforces the atmosphere, it is the dancer's body, alone or in combination with others, that gives visual expression to the impact of the surrounding environment on the character. Dance expression can provoke violent shifts of mood, too. In *Brigadoon,* dance carries the show from the lively and joyful country dance directly into the ritual mourning of the "Funeral Dance."

Among the revolutionary accomplishments of *Oklahoma!* was the discovery that the techniques of dance could be used to project the ideas of the book with no loss in dramatic credibility or suspension of

In the ballet "The Small House of Uncle Thomas" from *The King and I*, dance embodies the twin themes of slavery and oppression. (*Photo: The Museum of Modern Art Film Still Archives.*)

audience disbelief. If a song can be a scene, why can't a dance be a scene? Rodgers and Hammerstein assigned Act II, Scene 3, of *The King and I* to the ballet sequence "The Small House of Uncle Thomas," in which a stylized dance-narration of *Uncle Tom's Cabin* exhibits in microcosm the musical play's twin themes of slavery and oppression.

When musical theater collaborators explore the alternatives to dialogue for projecting the elements of the book, two possibilities occur: song and dance. Songs replace dialogue with compact language set to music; dance replaces dialogue with images of movement set to music. The advantage of dance? Movement forwards *action* more naturally than language. Multisecond dance sequences can equal multiminute book scenes in weight or scope of dramatic action. Consequently, dance accounts for the brevity of the action-packed *West Side Story* book, the most concise text in the repertory of great musicals.

Although both issue best from incongruity in dramatic situation, the true comedy of movement is more difficult to sustain on the stage than the conventional comedy of language. The reason: It is more in the nature of language to register the clash between the setup (expectation) and the punch (unsuspected fulfillment) that provokes the laughter response. To generate or elicit audience laughter, the choreographer must set up a visual situation and build into it an unsuspected visual response. Visual images are more difficult to achieve in surprise situations than language. A word can pop out anytime; not so a body or prop. No maker of dances has been more successful at comedy choreography than Jerome Robbins. You can study the phenomenon of dance comedy in his ballet *The Concert,* the "Keystone Cops Ballet" (*High Button Shoes*), the "Tevye's Dream" (*Fiddler on the Roof*).

When the cumulative development of a well-constructed book arrives at a moment of critical importance to the life of a musical show, the need usually arises to keep the audience there. Dance can extend that moment. It transports even the simplest point of development up and out, only to return it to the same place without recourse to repetition or reprise. Tony and Maria meet, dance, and fall in love, setting the plot on its inevitable course. When the dance ends, Tony and Maria return to the initial situation of having just met. Much has happened in that extended theatrical moment; yet nothing has happened in the plot beyond the fact that they've met. Used in this way, dance adds an emotional dimension without diverting the flow of the drama.

No device in the musical theater is more apt to generate the kinesthetic excitement that constitutes true spectacle than dance reinforced by sets, costumes, and lighting. Today, the American public is spectator to a variety of physical wonders in televised sports; the marvel of technology allows all to relish the virtuosity of athletes frozen in flight by instant replay. A nation of kinesthetic voyeurs accustomed to the increasing show-biz spectacle of sports merchandising, among many other outside influences, demands no less from the popular arts than it expects from the popular pastimes. The American musical theater has grown with its public. The dance spectacle that was once an attractive garnish now constitutes an essential ingredient in the preparation of the dish. In the most recent work of director-choreographers like Jerome Robbins, Bob Fosse, and Michael Bennett, spectacular theater dance makes a parallel, not a supplementary, contribution to the modern musical show.

Progression and pacing are part of what contribute to spectacle in a show, as well as the impact of the individual dances. Among the possible segments are the opening number, solo, duet, male or female ensemble, production number, ballet sequence, and crossover.

Although the opening number evolved from the "bring-on-the-girls-in-a-lively-routine" formula of early musical comedy, its place and function in the serious modern musical theater eschews cheap entertainment for the opportunity to demonstrate to the audience in physical terms the who, what, when, where, and how of the show to follow. The Jerome Robbins choreography for "Tradition" (*Fiddler on the Roof*) gives physical form to the show's immediate answer to each question. "Tradition" was conceived as a line dance that made extensive use of circle imagery. Robbins saw the religious and social tradition of the Jews as a circle that embraced all who believed and excluded all who did not. In addition, the content and staging of the number introduced the audience to the characters, theme, time, locale, and method of the entire show. Tevye, the mamas, papas, sons, and daughters of Anatevka constitute the who. The what: Jewish tradition. The when and where: Czarist Russia. The how: a story told primarily in the universal language of dance.

Performed by one person alone, the solo dance advances a single idea or character, as for example, in Cassie's solo, "The Music and the Mirror," from *A Chorus Line*. When the soloist represents the community, the solo dance speaks symbolically for all who matter in the world on the stage—"The Funeral Dance" from *Brigadoon* is a good example of this type. The solo dance offers an additional advantage to the choreographer: The special gifts of the best dancer can be used in patterns and combinations too difficult or ambitious for the ensemble.

With romantic love a staple in the musical theater, choreographers cannot afford to ignore the possibilities of the duet, a dance composition for two performers. What language can only signify of the physical character of a relationship, dance can establish through concrete images recognizable to the senses. Complementary body positions, harmonious movement, and affectionate gesture are themselves the expressions of romantic love, not merely symbols, like language, once removed from the fact. However, not all duets are amorous. Any relationship that permits physical expression invites choreographic treatment.

Audiences accept male or female ensemble dances as an inevitable dance category because human beings tend to congregate in sexually exclusive groups for special activities, social functions, and entertainment. Since conflict must delay the inevitable romantic resolution for nearly the entire length of most musical shows, male and female group dances offer opportunities for support, comment, or contrast to both sides of the battle between the sexes. They also adumbrate period

Dance, music, lyrics, set, costumes, and orchestration create this spectacular moment from the film *Rosalie*, 1937. (*Photo: The Museum of Modern Art Film Still Archives.*)

atmosphere, in reflecting the masculine and feminine styles of different eras.

In the production number, the entire dance ensemble contributes to purposeful spectacle. The production number represents the choreographer's most collaborative effort as dance joins music, lyrics, performers, set, costumes, and orchestration in a joyous and full musical theater moment.

Dance becomes the ally of plot in the ballet sequence. This type of dance can precipitate action ("The Dream Ballet" in *Oklahoma!*), comment on situation ("Ballet Sequence" in *West Side Story*), or advance an argument ("Small House of Uncle Thomas" in *The King and I*). When the choreographer must devise dances that divert the audience from unavoidable technical problems, these brief dances performed before a downstage drop curtain are called crossovers.

When the time comes to choreograph, no one method prevails. However, a good bet would be to start with the dance idea and the music.

Paul Draper said it best: "A dance is made of a series of steps, but a series of steps do not make a dance." Successful dance grows out of an idea that shapes all choreographic decisions on steps, attitudes, gestures, movement, and style. Although public perception of the show choreographer's job generally focuses on the practical duties of inventing steps, the task of coming up with a sound theoretical basis for the dance represents the most valuable contribution choreographers can make to the dance-making process. A stage choreographer should use the collaborative process to determine what the dance must say or do during its brief, scheduled appearance on the show's performance itinerary. Temptations to do otherwise abound. If the popular musical stage courts audience approval, then why not give the public what it wants—flash, virtuosity, and the old razzle-dazzle? Why not? Because shabby theatricality in stage dance belongs to the past; the present and the future belong to raised standards, growing dance influence, and artistic integrity. A cautionary note: Once the dance idea has been determined, believe in it. Otherwise the rehearsal process and its product will fall short of expectations.

If the concept of a show bestows the dance idea, then its music escorts it. Show dancing celebrates its special relationship to music. Whether you dance to the music, on the music, or against the music, the music will be there as an aural referent to just what is going on in the dance. Do not expect the master choreographers to follow the music note for note, measure for measure, musical phrase for musical phrase. Whereas the earliest dance directors aimed for steps that were the visual equivalent of the attendant sound, modern practice favors the view of music as an analogous and complementary part of the dance. Music makes its presence felt structurally—since musical form often influences dance form; rhythmically—since rhythm provides the basis in time for sound and movement; and emotionally—as melody and harmony aurally color the working dance images. As music is to words is music to dance: It cannot declare, define, or denote but only suggest. But in suggestion lies the secret, the charm, the power. What more apt an appeal to the imagination can there be than the power to suggest in a performance art? It is music's power to arouse associative meanings that draws the choreographer to it; it is then the choreographer's job to translate a personal vision and response to it into the design, steps, and style of the dance. Choreography that leans too heavily on the music loses its capacity to astonish. Choreography that belabors the obvious compromises an audience's ability to respond to it enthusiastically. Acting can and does rely on literal physical projection; dancing should rely on a stylized alternative. Musical shows are not natural phenomena. Choreography that duplicates realistic behavior usually fails in a presentational medium. Recognizing the artifice in their situation, show dance choreographers work hard to create an immediate, early impression. Kinetic communication begins with the dancing's initial contact with the audience, and those early impressions often form a prejudicial relationship that can color whatever happens between the two later. Audiences in a darkened theater can make judgments long before their decisions are registered in applause. Show dance choreography must begin the best possible first impression. In this business, few who fail merit a second chance.

12

The Stage, Film, and Video

Of the five principal areas of commercial dance—nightclub, commercial television, the musical stage, film, and video, no two are more visible, popular, and productive today than film and video. The reasons are clear. Film and video are the adopted media of the young. These media communicate with a physical, visual, and emotional intensity that mirrors youthful preoccupations. Video particularly allows America's children to see their songs and imitate their songsters; that is, to share more intimately in the aural and visual life of their idols. Film and video dancing reach as many as they do because the youth market has been a formidable force in American merchandising during the last decade, and deep-rooted tendencies in both media tend to shun art and court popularity. As the Broadway and Hollywood dance director LeRoy Prinz put it nearly forty years ago: "In screen dancing, we cater to the masses, not to the classes." Although sincere and impressive attempts at filmed dance art do exist—Gene Kelly's *Invitation to the Dance*, for instance—show dancing for the camera, with the exception of artfully rendered versions of stage shows, remains today what it was in the era of the dance directors—a lightweight, lowbrow entertainment activity subject to popular trends and a commitment to immediate gratification for its own sake. Film and video cater to the masses, and the masses dance for pleasure. If much of that pleasure derives from the kinetic expression of raw sex and youthful energy, then it is precisely these qualities that the public will look for in commercial entertainments. Then, when faced with the choice between a commercial entertainment and an artistic statement, the majority in the screen dance audience opt for the former.

191

Obviously, major philosophical and practical differences separate live show dancing from its filmed equivalent, and it is these differences that give choreographers, dancers, and audiences a real choice between substantially different professional and entertainment alternatives.

1. Stage dancing happens within a three-dimensional medium; film and video flatten the dance and the dancers into images of length and width only. Stage dancing has the advantage here in that the human body, itself a three-dimensional instrument, complements (as it moves in) an appropriate space. Onstage, the dancer and the dance can make use of all angles and directions just as they allow the audience to focus at will on whatever element in the dance most appeals to it. In stage dancing, audiences select the images of their own enjoyment. In film

In film dance, the camera selects what the audience will see, as in this long shot of Ginger Rogers and Fred Astaire in *Top Hat*, 1938. (*Photo: Theater Collection, Free Library of Philadelphia.*)

and video, the camera makes that selection. Stage choreographers who tyrannize dancers cannot tyrannize audiences as do the film choreographers who select what the audience will be allowed to see. That option offers mixed blessings. When choreographers attempt to film three-dimensional stage dancing from an audience perspective, the results can be as dismal as any translation from one medium to another without attendant adjustments. When choreographers adapt, or better still re-create, movement for the camera, the results can be as admirable or as stimulating as the best work of Busby Berkeley, Fred Astaire, and Gene Kelly.

2. Stage dancing is the live entertainment that movies and video can only simulate on film. Movement affirms life in a biological and psychological sense. The joy of walking, running, leaping, and turning derives from the mover's kinetic awareness of the life-invested body performing such moves. Whatever the quality of intent, stage dancing celebrates the physical, visceral fact of life before audiences who are themselves alive. The community achieved and the bond established is more than communicative or aesthetic, it is deeply human. With repeated live performances, of course, come the prospects of change, variation, even error. The very perfection of the filmed dance sequence actually removes it from the real world where activity admits to no such perfection. The "frozen" nature of filmed dance sequences precludes many opportunities open to stage dancers, dancing, and audiences. Stage choreography in successful shows undergoes numerous changes in casting that allow dancers to reinterpret the choreography, allow the steps and movement to take on a new look, and allow the audience to experience new bodies and new values brought to the old and familiar routines. In this sense stage dances have many lives, lives that extend over many years and spread out among even more dancers. After the original cast departs, the show is brought to life again by the second, third, or fourth cast, the London production, all road companies, and major revivals. Except for some of the original film choreography for *Singin' in the Rain* retained for the stage adaptation, variations of interpretation and performance of the successful film dances of Fred Astaire, Gene Kelly, and others have not been available to audiences in any medium.

3. Stage dances must be executed effectively in their entirety at all performances. Film and video dances can be assembled by reshooting and editing, and, if necessary, reworked technically into dances that could never be performed live in their entirety. Of course, the practice and habits of filming dance change with time and fashion. Today, a

John Travolta's dancing in *Staying Alive*, 1983, owed as much to editing as to the movement skills of the performer. (*Photo: The Museum of Modern Art Film Still Archives.*)

John Travolta dance for *Staying Alive* owes as much to accomplished editing as to the movement skills of the performer. Compare the extensive and intrusive editing of recent film and video dances to any of the classic dances of Fred Astaire and Ginger Rogers. Note how long the couple dance together before the camera in extended sequences. Consider the preparation, rehearsal, and virtuosity required to sustain such excellence over considerable periods of time. Consider, too, how the dance viewed by the film audience represents a fairly accurate account of the performers' ability and talent. The camera never expected Fred and Ginger to do what they could not. Since so many current film and video stars cannot do, the technical staff and the camera do it for them. As musical recordings can be mixed and manufactured in a studio to sound as they never could in live performance, so can staging and dancing be manufactured by camera work and editing. This is not to disparage the practice, since film dance never intends to be or to be compared with its live counterpart. One longs for the good old days of film dancing, however, and the attitude and approach to dance that led Fred Astaire to assert, "Either the camera will dance, or I will. But both of us at the same time—that won't work." That attitude persists still in stage dancing, where no technology exists to cover the live dancer. Where film work can tolerate, even assist, the attractive nondancer, stage dancing demands stamina, flexibility, suppleness, technique, and talent. Stage dancers so endowed take the genuine risks that accompany virtuosity. The option of additional retakes in film reduces and in some cases eliminates all risk and, unfortunately, the highly charged response to it that often makes for great performances.

4. Although stage dance profits from live performance, its setting and decor remain tied and therefore limited to the conventions of the stage. Filmed dances specialize in opening up the environment for dance to anything, anyplace, anywhere that can be filmed. Consider the opportunities exercised during the filming of *West Side Story*. Here, dancing in the actual streets of New York City was achieved by filming actual dancing in the streets of New York City. Whereas stage choreographers like Jerome Robbins believe that their best dance work has been done with simple sets and dramatic lighting, ever so appropriate to theatrical conventions, decades of memorable film choreography attest to the importance of spectacular settings and environments to its dancing. The Busby Berkeley routines were not displayed before simple sets. The Astaire-Rogers backgrounds set the standard and the tone for lavish 1930s chic. Only a Hollywood sound stage of herculean proportions could have housed the overwhelming space, sets, lighting equipment, and cast of the "Broadway Melody" production number from *Singin' in the Rain*. Show dance has always traded on spectacle, only the spectacle in film has always been more spectacular than in any other show business medium.

5. The intimacy made possible by the camera highlights all flaws in the dancing and the dancer. Film so directs and concentrates audience focus that it exaggerates every movement and announces every flaw. Clever stage makeup, lighting, and costuming might disguise facial and physical liabilities that would never go undetected by the camera. Consequently, film and video dancing favor the slim, beautiful, perfectly proportioned dancer over the average-looking, versatile technician. Dancing ability alone cannot guarantee success in film work—witness the undersubscribed Hollywood career of Gwen Verdon. Hollywood dance director Billy Daniels addressed the problem early on. Said he in *Dance*

Busby Berkeley relied on spectacular settings and costumes for routines like this one from *Gold Diggers of 1933.* (*Photo: The Museum of Modern Art Film Still Archives.*)

Only a Hollywood sound stage of Herculean proportions could have accommodated the movement for this production number from *Singin' In the Rain.* (*Photo: The Museum of Modern Art Film Still Archives.*)

The spectacle in dance films has always been more spectacular than in any other show business medium, as typified in this scene from *Rosalie*, 1937. (*Photo: The Museum of Modern Art Film Still Archives.*)

Magazine February: "Since the public demands acting ability and personality in a male or female lead, it will not accept a dancer unless he can couple these qualities with a gift for dancing." Today, the widespread use of a dancing double relieves the movie star from the need to dance. Did the considerable audience for *Flashdance* know or even care that the dancing was not actually performed by the person who seemed to be performing it?

6. Since film permits worldwide release for its entertainments, dancers seek out the medium for its widest possible career exposure. On a given night, a dancer in a Broadway show can be seen by that audience only; on a given night, the image of that dancer on the screen can be seen anywhere and by as many audiences allowed by the number of available prints for that film. For this reason quality dancers and choreographers have been lured to Hollywood from Broadway. Among the dancer-actors: Fred Astaire, from vaudeville, musical comedy, and revue; Gene Kelly, from *Pal Joey*; and John Travolta, from *Over Here*. Among the dance directors and director-choreographers: Robert Alton, Jack Cole, and Bob Fosse.

Filmed dance as in *Staying Alive,* 1983, favors the beautiful, well-proportioned performer over the versatile if plain technician. (*Photo: The Museum of Modern Art Film Still Archives.*)

   7. Whereas film offers the dancer maximum professional exposure, stage dancing offers its community the opportunity for nightly exposure before tryout audiences whose reactions to the dancing and the dancers can be measured. Between the rehearsal studio and opening night, weeks or even months of audience feedback can modify, alter, or eliminate a dance. Out of town and preview allow a choreographer to be wrong or a dancer to be unready. Usually, a live dance that is finished but ineffective can be fixed; a film dance that is finished and filmed cannot. In Hollywood there is no such thing as the preview process or an out-of-town tryout. Gower Champion once confessed his frustration with the medium:

> In pictures, barring expensive retakes, a dance routine as well as a scene, is either good or it is out. To the creative mind working in a visual field, this can be a source of extreme frustration. . . . In Hollywood you have a longer rehearsal and preparation period, but you need them because you have to be right the first time.

   Critics and choreographers who speak of "cinematized" film dancing refer to the obtrusively technical methods of creating film dance glorified

in movies like *Flashdance, Footloose,* and *Staying Alive.* Whereas earlier
film dancing recorded blocks of extended, largely unedited movement,
cinematized dancing represents a composite of brief, filmed kinetic effects
sensationally photographed and blended into a tempting meal of dance
scraps for the modern, with-it, junk-food dance audience. If the camera
makes cinematized dancing possible, then one can say that recent films
are really rolling those cameras as they explore the unique potential of
film as a dance medium. Where stage dancing suffers from the fixed
position of the audience in relation to the dancers on the stage, film
dance thrives on the possibilities of camera movement, angles, close-ups,
long shots, special effects, and dissolves. Because they are alive and move
before constructed backdrops, the dancers in stage musicals always seem
more real than their environment. Film makes the dancers as artificial
and two-dimensional as their environment, if not more so. Since film
audiences need not be spared consciousness of the camera, modern film
dancing luxuriates in all the tricks of angle and editing peculiar to the
medium. Once, Hollywood photographed dance with one camera from
a single position. No concession was made to adapt the dance to the best

The camera accounts for trick routines like Fred Astaire's ceiling dance
from *Royal Wedding,* 1951. (*Photo:
The Museum of Modern Art Film Still
Archives.*)

Gene Kelly and Cyd Charisse close-up during the "Broadway Melody" sequence from *Singin' In The Rain*. (*Photo: The Museum of Modern Art Film Still Archives.*)

interest of the medium. The product offered a photographic record of the dance but little else. Recognition of camera mobility has long since made the fixed-seat angle obsolete, opening the viewer and the dance to a variety of perspectives and an immediacy of presence impossible in a theater. Today's film choreographers design dances to be more like a rapid succession of pictures than the kinetically organized movement experience we encounter in ballet, modern dance, and Broadway shows. The succession can involve long shots and close-ups, lines and angles, footwork and decor. Yet all must appear to be part of the dance, just as steps, combinations, movement, and composition come together in a dance for the stage. Intelligent editing becomes as much a part of the choreography as the steps. Dangers abound. When directors set the camera back far enough to include the entire ensemble, then the dancers become too small to be effective; when directors set the camera too close, limbs, torso, and facial expression profit at the expense of the choreographic design. Good film choreography accounts for the focus of the camera. If the focus is on the principal, excessive background movement detracts. If the principal and a partner move, then the camera might move if the objective is to keep the couple within the camera frame. The stationary camera not only makes such standard formations as the straight line across the stage unbearable, but all dancing that depends on footwork as well.

Although film and video dancing share most of the properties that distinguish them from their stage counterparts, a few differences prevail. The size of the screen in film offers images of dancing that are larger than life; the size of the video screen offers images of dancing that are considerably smaller. Consequently, choreography must adapt, particularly in the areas of composition, steps, and movement direction. Predictably, video dancing glorifies isolation. Small but definite movement suits the small screen. Special effects suit it even more, since video choreography deals in images and moving images need not be human. Stage directors have choreographed scenery for decades. Why shouldn't video choreographers manipulate its frames as well? Because video dancing serves the song only, its material need not serve any context other than immediate self-interest. In a sense, video staging resembles the vaudeville routine designed to provoke immediate audience approval within a prescribed time limit. Within the format, a Bob Fosse–like jazz

Good film choreography, as in *Rosalie,* 1937, accounts for the focus of the camera. If the focus is on the principal, excessive background movement would detract. (*Photo: The Museum of Modern Art Film Still Archives.*)

Michael Kidd's choreography for *Seven Brides for Seven Brothers* exploited movement suited to the wide screen. (*Photo: The Museum of Modern Art Film Still Archives.*)

style prevails. Most movement tends to be torso-centered, swift, and precise—rarely aerial, syncopated, and sexy. Understanding the demands of the small screen, video choreographers concentrate on small, sharp, angular steps usually derived from shoulder, hip, and head isolations. Turns in place work best. Groupings share the stylistic considerations afforded the soloist. Usually, the camera moves when the group moves. Traveling steps accommodate the camera. If the camera seriously compromises horizontal movement in film dance, it all but annihilates it in video. Movement choreographed directly toward the camera works better. As the soloist or grouping travel back to front, their presence grows dramatically within an already limited frame. One such moment in Michael Jackson's "Thriller" video illustrates the point.

In spite of technical and aesthetic limitations, video dance thrives; it is popular, accessible, youth-oriented, and as accurate a measure as any of our popular culture today.

INDEX